Jonny Fluffypunk is the stage ~~~~~~~~~~~~~~~~~~~~~~~~~~~~~~ ın
Stephen Harman Se~~~~~~~~~~~~~~~~~~~~~~~~~~~~~~~~~~~~~~~ h
earlier in his 'career'
Wreckless Eric has s
and everywhere for ne
sells books from a batt~~~~~~~~~~~~~~~~~~~~~~~~~~~~~~~~~~n,
no-fi, hi-art DIY punk ~~~~~~~~~~~~~~~~~~~~~.....ıy committed to low
production values, gaffer tape is his king and the shaky camera,
the glue gun and the cardboard prop are his best friends. To
plagiarise Mike Watt of Minutemen, *he jams econo*.

Poundland
Rimbaud

To John

Jonny Fluffypunk

*love
Jonny
xx*

Burning Eye

This edition published by Burning Eye Books 2016

www.burningeye.co.uk
@burningeyebooks

Burning Eye Books
15 West Hill, Portishead, BS20 6LG

ISBN 978 1 90913 660 1

For Katherine, Ianto and Percy

Jesting decides great things
Stronglier, and better oft than earnest can

Horace's *Satires*, translated by John Milton

CONTENTS

POUNDLAND RIMBAUD

THINGS BY

JONNY FLUFFYPUNK

FULLY ANNOTATED

Poetry is a calling. A vocation. My ambition for as long as I can remember.

As a young man, I *told* them;

I said, *I want to be A POET. I want words to spill from my mouth and take root in the windswept souls of rebels on the barricades; I want words to spill from my mouth and touch the hearts of impossible women.*

Women who otherwise I would never get to touch.

Anywhere.

And they said, *You do that, son. You do that.*

And I looked them in the eyes and said, *I will. BY CHRIST I WILL*, and I laughed at the whole wild beauty of it all and they asked me to keep my voice down as I was disturbing the other jobseekers.

HOW TO DO
PERFORMANCE POETRY.

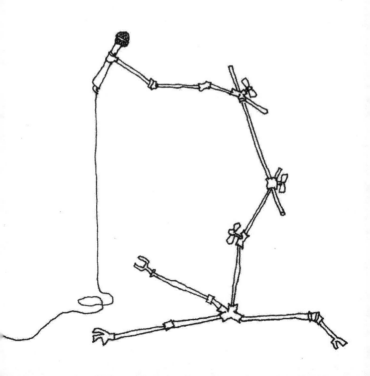

WE GO TOGETHER

with notes and guidance for creating effective romantic poetry

We go together[1]
like cricket bats go with leather balls
like chirpy cockneys go with market stalls
like Mark E Smith goes with the Fall [2]
we go together.

We go together like leylines go with Glastonbury Tor[3]
like exaggerating and completely untrue graffiti
about me and Sharon Stacey

---

1   Strong start! No lack of commitment here, ladies. *Show* you mean business.

2   Hipster reference, this. Combine it with the cricketing reference and the hint that I make my on-street purchases from salt-of-the-earth proletarians rather than corduroy-clad pseudo-'farmer' ponces flogging quail's egg paté to moneyed idiots, and she'll start to get the picture of a simple, solid guy who spends his time seeing through bullshit, listening to jagged art-punk and sending cakes made with thriftily-sourced ingredients to the commentary team of Test Match Special. Well-rounded.

3   Wow. All the above and spiritual, too?

goes with public lavatory doors[4]
we go together.

We go together
like Marmite goes with buttered toast
like seagulls go with English coast
like gravy goes with Sunday roast[5]

---

4   Not the best example, but never be afraid to use your poetry to
    confront injustice, to right wrongs, or simply to get even with
    wankers. Remember, you're a poet. You're painting pictures,
    but with words. I'm always aware that my every poem – even
    a love poem like this – is potentially Goya's Execution of the
    Defenders of Madrid with me as the white-shirted, defiant
    innocent in the centre, arms outstretched, Christ-like, as
    Napoleon's lackeys unload their rifles into my noble forehead.
    The wankers might think they've done me down, but history
    is on my side. And, in this case, the recipient of this poem will
    know I don't suffer any crap.

5   A risky tactic, comparing (even obliquely) a woman, or one's
    relationship with a woman, to foodstuffs. Or even mentioning
    foodstuffs. In this stanza I've recklessly gone for good old
    love-it-or-hate-it Marmite and a solid, filling Sunday dinner,
    with Yorkshire puddings, but then for me poetry has always
    been about danger. Also, with a yeast extract included in the
    analogy, the more over-sensitive woman might conclude that
    I'm hinting to the world she's got a candida infection. It's a
    gamble.

like list poems more than most
go with weak lines that help maintain the rhyme
    scheme.[6]

We go together
like sweets go with strangers
like messiahs go with mangers
at least at birth[7]
we go together
like Mother goes with Earth

---

6   Deconstruction of the poem from within the poem! Hip, well-rounded, romantic AND post-modern. Also handily reveals that, as an artist, I'm well aware of the stylistic naïveté and constraints of this particular poetic form; that really, I'm above this sort of simplistic shit but, hey, *I'm not above having fun.*

7   Note the subtle 'ramping up' of the analogies. I'm coming on stronger. I started out comparing the relationship to a cricket bat; now I'm comparing it to the birth of Jesus. Doing it the other way round wouldn't have the same impact, unless of course I were attempting to pull an atheist with a season ticket for Trent Bridge. Which, funnily enough, I have attempted.

like self goes with worth[8]
we go together.

We go together
like fill-your-plate-for-a-fiver restaurants
go with rather tiny plates
like gridlock goes with motor cars
and getting in a state
we go together.

We go together like a bike
goes with pedals
like a soldier goes with medals
like beer goes with hops
like corruption goes with cops
like rampant attraction goes with
a woman with a feral armpit smell
and a Laura Ashley top
we go together

---

8   This is where performance poetry comes into its own, lines
    like this. You can change the whole impact, the whole direction
    of the piece, simply by a subtle change in your delivery. Play
    around with it! If I performed this line in a strong, decisive
    fashion, I'd no doubt attract a strong, decisive woman. As it
    is, I tend to plump for a hint of wavering uncertainty and thus
    keep attracting girls who want to mother me, feeding me up and
    knitting me many attractive woollen items.

like effective romantic poetry
goes with knowing

when to stop.[9]

---

9   This is the killer final stanza. This is where I lay my cards on the table, take it or leave it. Good poetry follows the maxim of show, don't tell, so my seemingly random choice of analogies is actually a coded flagging up of my hobbies and interests. She'll hear these lines and subconsciously she'll get the message that I'm environmentally aware, that I'm not averse to a bit of fighting and drinking, that I'm anti-authoritarian, that I don't give a shit for gender stereotypes yet at the same time I'm sensitive enough to notice the new frock she's wearing and, last but not least, that I'm self-aware and know the value of silence.

Now, go and write your own.

SIX SHORT SCENES
FROM A TOUR DIARY.

THEY SHOULD HAVE BEEN BIGGER THAN THE BEATLES

So I'm packing poems, pants and paired socks into an artisanal kitbag handcrafted from rough tweed and patterned with faded dreams, and I'm avoiding the gaze of my electric guitar, leant untouched against the wall since God knows when, steeped in dust and recrimination. Two hundred quid she cost, and that was twenty-five years ago. *And* I bought the flight case, too; the heavy-duty leads. We were meant to go places.

There should at least have been a tour. There should've been *many* tours. There should've been a tatty Transit van, driven by a drug-dispensing drummer who never spoke. The bass player, he should've been a no-bullshit mother hen, gaffer-taping that village hall bookings secretary to the weathervane of the Baptist church, hanging him by his ankles 'til he coughed up our agreed fee. That bassist should've been shooing me outside as I expounded our revolutionary manifesto to a wide-eyed angel in a hand-knit tank top and sturdy outdoor shoes. *Plenty of action in the next town*, he'd have said. *That's* what it was supposed to be like. A *gang*. A gang and guitars and gigs and girls. Instead it's like this: poesy and gazing out train windows and a guitar that just sits staring at the wall as I throw an extra pair of socks in the bag, just to be on the safe side.

That guitar.

Look, you know what it's like when you flatshare with someone you've always really fancied, and you move in all your books and records and hopes and expectations and then suddenly, one morning, you wake up with the cold, sad certainty that it's just not going to happen; that somehow you've missed that moment when it all could have blossomed, become *something more*, something big, something beautiful?

Yes?

Well, that.

HEROES
GIG / LIBRARY / STOKE-ON-TRENT

The lady double-checks the audience
has emptied their bladders;
the stairlift's playing up again
and *no one wants a repeat of last time*.

Well, that's one I've got on you, Lou Reed.
I bet Iggy never gets told to flag up the
induction loop for the hard of hearing.

And just try to picture Bowie
as they show *him* to the fridge
where they've put the rider –

a Tesco Meal Deal sandwich
and a Meal Deal bottle of water.

The crisps, he'd say, coming on all diva.
Where's the Meal Deal crisps?

Picture *his* face, when informed *the crisps
are for the support act...*

I FOUND THAT ESSENCE RARE
POETRY TAKEAWAY / GOODS SHED / STROUD

I am sat in a little booth.

I do poems for people. They tell me what they want.
I ask them questions. I do them a poem.

I do one for a kid whose stuffed unicorn likes
interstellar adventure and smoky bacon crisps.
You have to mention the crisps.

I do one for a beautiful woman
who feels the need to apologise to her daughter.

I do one for a couple on their anniversary. He tells me
their first date was in Birmingham and wants me to
capture how magical it felt, him waltzing her all round
the Bullring. *Bollocks*, she says, *it was Wetherspoons
in Cov.*

I do one for an old lady who once sugared her
underskirts and jived in milk bars with a boyfriend the
spit of Billy Fury.

I do one for a lady who misses her dead cat.

I do one for a man who misses his dead wife.

Do one about me! Go on! a lady says.
I explain that I'm on my lunch break;
that I can barely move my wrist from

all the furious scribbling.

Look, your sign says you do instant poems for people
and I'm leaving in ten minutes
and I WANT A POEM.

My reply is pure fucking poetry –
other people would win prizes for such *directness*,
such *economy of language*.

THE IMAGE HAS CRACKED
GIG / PUB / ROBERTSBRIDGE, EAST SUSSEX

When that old boy pulled his lighter from his coat
and held it aloft as I blazed
into an extended sequence
about the death of my dog,

well, that's when I just closed my eyes
and knew that this was what
I'd always been waiting for.

And yes, of course, we all know *now*
he was just hunting for his meds –
colitis, I think it was. Maybe angina.

But still, for those short minutes;

those perfect golden minutes.

(WE'RE JUST A) MINOR THREAT
WORKSHOP / LIBRARY / BROWNHILLS, WALSALL

What is it you do exactly?
says the stone-faced librarian
with the air of having events
foisted upon her she
can do without.

Words, I say.
I do words.

I bring words to share.
Words that will leave my mouth,
take to the air and dance in the ears
of this small audience of library users.
And I explain that
when we have feasted
on the proffered poetry cake
I will tell the audience that they –
they are the ingredients
with which we will make more.
Together, we will bake FRESH POETRY.
We will create.
We will celebrate these people.
These lives.
This library.
This town.
There will be joy.

And though she informs me

that people in Brownhills
really don't like that sort of thing,
the librarian's hard face smiles.

A librarian smiles.

A Wembley moment for poetry.

THE MAN WHOSE HEAD EXPANDED
GIG / BLUE WALNUT CAFÉ / TORQUAY

At the merch table
I sell a book to a lady
who says I remind her of her son.

I nod, awkwardly.

She nods back
and says she hopes her son
bucks his ideas up and
pulls his bloody finger out.

SELFIES.

PORTRAIT OF THE ARTIST AT THE COALFACE
OF THE NEW ROCK 'N' ROLL

I blame it on that Kate Tempest,
borne aloft on the shoulders of public acclaim
like a tiny rhyming elf

is how I explain all of this
to the lady from the literature festival
as we speed through the streets
of the small Suffolk market town
in her clapped-out Micra

and tonight I think I killed it;
the book club ladies sighed and nodded
and the girl in the tweed trench coat
with eyes as dusty and inviting
as the windows of second-hand bookshops
slammed her head to the rhythm of rustled paper
and awkward silence

before we all melted off into the night
like poems melting back to raw ink

and now back at the B&B
the lit fest lady cracks open a yoghurt,
lines up the Earl Grey slammers
as the girl with the bookshop eyes
leads me to the bed
and as the Nurofen starts kicking in
we lower heads and lick Hobnob crumbs
from the plump stomach of a naked librarian.

PORTRAIT OF THE ARTIST AS AN ANIMAL
RIGHTS EXTREMIST

In this one it's Wednesday; hunt sabs social.
We're scattered round my flat's front room.

The Cat with Electrodes Stuck in Its Head
stares down from its poster on the wall;

You enjoy your cider, mate,
don't mind me. Go ahead.

Fuck off, cat. My hand is enjoying
the hard-won warmth of Rachel's thigh;
I'm gazing at her slender white neck,
the bit just where it disappears under her pink hair.
Like a swan with its head up a flamingo's arse,
said Phil, when I tried to explain its beauty. He's so
Class War; laughs that I've *become a bunny hugger*
as he scoffs proletarian chicken nuggets in an
unrepentant leather jacket. I guess
I won't be seeing much of him in future

So I'm sat here on the sofa, next to Rach,
my ear thrilling to the click of tongue piercing
against teeth as she addresses the room.
She's off about soya milk again;
how Provamel's best, no question.
Never Alpro and NEVER from Holland & Barrett.
Owned by Dewhurst. Bastards...

And I think YES!
That's the sort of passion that inspired me to run home
from the George those long six weeks ago,
grinning through a haze of April rain and
ethically-approved ale, desperate
to wrench open the fridge; to throw the Lurpak
in the bin in a fit of righteous clarity.
To sort my life out. To take a *stand*.

Rach knows where she stands on *everything*.
Some people are like that.
Don't know what it's like to waver.
Never go to sleep certain t*hat's the last time I ever...*
then wake up to find the feeling gone.
They can *always* be bothered, and
I'd love to be that definite about things –
to have the words *no compromise*
muttered in the same breath as my name,
but how can you trust a man
who has the full set of Crass albums
but who can be lured from the path
of righteousness by the unholy
smell of a kebab?

So when Davey strides in from the kitchen
holding aloft a tin of creamed rice pudding,
there's not much I can say.

I didn't read the small print won't do here;
there's *always* time to read the small print

when animals are suffering
and no one will be impressed that it's because
I just rushed round Sainsbury's that afternoon;
that I needed to get back and record the last three
tracks on Rach's compilation tape before the birthday
buffet at the vegan Indian. That I'm just a bit crap like
that.

And so the conversation just stops dead;
Rachel's soft thigh is snatched away;
the tongue piercing clicks one last time
like the snapped neck of a hanged man

and the Cat with Electrodes Stuck in Its Head
stares down from its poster on the wall, triumphant.

PORTRAIT OF THE ARTIST AS A YOUNG VIRGIN

I would dread going 'up' the village, past the nursery and the school, toward the recreation ground and, though they were of little interest to me, the pubs. Going 'up' the village entailed the danger of going past the foot of Meadow Cottages, the council estate of my mother's warnings: a feckless Sodom of lemonade and ringworm, white bread and ITV. Most dangerous were the young ladies. Michaela and Alison were their names. Alison a pale, huge and terrible object encased in a tartan overcoat and topped with a frizzy mane of dark Pre-Raphaelite hair, like a poodle mounting a giant bagpipe. Michaela dark and cold, thin-lipped and with an air of the gypsy, more bare-knuckle fighting than mischievous twinkle. They would haunt the lane that wound through the centre of the village, through the centre of my world, pouncing from the shadows of driveways, from behind trees or from the cock-scrawled cave of the bus shelter. Pouncing on easy prey.

Do you like girls, boy? You ever kissed a girl? You want to know what a girl feels like, boy?
Has a girl ever touched your winkle, boy? You ever seen a fanny, boy? Rubbed a tit? You bummed anyone?

These, I knew, must be *feminists*: brazen, forward women of the type that would upset my father, reclining on his chaise longue and spluttering oaths into his Horlicks as they paraded their liberated viewpoints on the Hades of the Fourth Channel.

These two knew their terrible power, and they flaunted it. Yes, they frightened me. But they were strangely alluring, too. *Feminists*. The very word reeked of the new tomorrow; of the new dawn that was beginning to probe insistent golden fingers onto my dull horizon, a dawn borne on the sleeves of anarchist punk records.

But this was grown-up stuff. My Saturdays still belonged to the platform end; my veins pumped diesel and my heart beat faster only for locomotives, packed lunches and scribbled numbers. In a year's time, things would be different. I would have crossed the line. A girl would have shown me her breasts on the Euston–Glasgow overnight, and though prudence would have caused me to gaze at the magical orbs only as reflections in the dim light of the compartment window, it would have been with a longing hitherto foreign to me. An hour later, outside Carlisle station, drunk on new experience, I would have bitten into my first kebab.

I would be of the world of men.

STUFF.

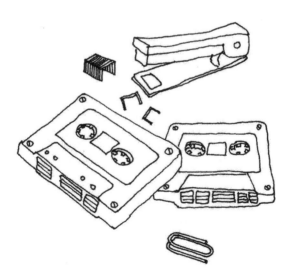

ACCIDENT & EMERGENCY

Tonight, I've invited her over.
I run the boat engine
to heat the water, shower,
then spend a quarter-hour
faffing over trousers.

I trash the cupboard
hunting out a vase.
I put out flowers.

I wax the old moustache,
crack open a bottle of Blossom Hill red,
ignite some vile aromatherapy candle
and turn off the lights.

Then the door crashes open
and she thunders in.

The highlight of my fucking day
was squeezing urine
from the bladder of a corpse,

and she goes for the wine,
but not in the way I'd hoped.

WHEN I DRAW THE MAP OF HEAVEN, X WILL MARK THE GREASY SPOON[10]

There are 486,752 love poems in the world
and I am sat in this café
at the same table we sat
as the owner hums along
to a phone-in racist on *Jeremy Vine*.

I've got paper and an envelope
and I am trying to write love poem #486,753 –
a love poem for you –
but the paper stays blank
and the words will not come.

But my breakfast does come –
a breakfast number five

---

10   Of course, as a boho *artiste* I have had to make myself thoroughly
      au fait with modern café culture; I'm able to convincingly order
      a soya milk option on a tall latte and dither over the gluten-free
      flapjacks. However, my heart is not in it and I'd far prefer to be
      soiling myself in an establishment where a soya milk option on
      a latte is impossible, not least because a latte is impossible. An
      establishment where it's instant, *or fuck off*. An establishment
      where feral children driven insane by blue squash from plastic
      cartons bully defenceless grandparents for twenty pence for the
      Thomas the Tank Engine ride. An establishment where you can
      feast for less than four quid and if you don't take your plate
      back to the hatch after you'll get a well-deserved earful for
      your lack of manners.

just like back then –
a breakfast to fall in love with.
A breakfast to fall in love over.

Two egg, two sausage, beans,
bubble, toms and mushrooms,
toast of course, a cup of instant
stirred with stained spoon chained
to crusted Formica.

These eggs are twin suns blazing
on the scarred blue sky of plate,
the sausages are your taut thighs
lolling beside the beans' hot pool,
the bubble is our own desert island,
mushrooms like nipples,
the two plum tomatoes are testicles
heavy with promise,
ketchup like pounding blood.[11]

I plunge the blank and wordless paper
into the hot poem of this breakfast;
wallow it in the lusty riot
of grease and yolk and sauce.

---

11 This is poetic licence. I would, of course, be having brown
sauce. The sauce of champions..

I kiss a cold crust of toast
and I pop it all in the envelope
and I post it to you

You who will open it.
You who will understand.
You who will breathe deep of this breakfast;
will know just what it means to want
to share a breakfast this perfect.
You who will cup the cold crust to your breast
like a heartbeat.

BAPS

On the A371 four miles south of Shepton Mallet:
two laybys. Two catering trailers,
one each side of the carriageway.

We're heading north,
so swing in to join the throng
at Kylie's Big Baps.

Kylie's doing good. Her griddle sizzles;
she gamely flips the slabs of beef,
flirts with thickset truckers who squirt on sauce,
napkin juices off their chins.

Southbound, it's a different story –
the Butty Boys stand idle, twiddling thumbs,
contemplating their miscalculation,

their soft buns unbuttered,
their plump sausages wilting.

DELICATESSEN[12]

It was a thrill when we heard, gazing into the froth on our halves: *He's bought himself a delicatessen.*

That's what you'd do if life went right. If the book took off. If the TV people got in touch and the bald producer with the moist handshake stopped saying *remind me of your name?* If Jill from NatWest came on the phone, with an attitude and interest rate to suit enhanced financial status. You'd buy a delicatessen.

You wouldn't *work* in it; you wouldn't sit up nights googling cheap wholesale suppliers of puy lentil

---

12 This poem was inspired by receiving the news – whilst sat in a Bath pub nursing a half of whatever real ale was on special offer and sharing a bag of crisps – that poet Joe Dunthorne, member of East Anglian 'poetry boyband' Aisle 16 and author of the novel *Submarine*, had accumulated sufficient disposable income from his written endeavours to buy himself a delicatessen, seemingly on a whim. The news was sketchy and unsubstantiated, but enough to plunge those present into fervent reverie. This was *one of us*. One of us who now, it seemed, had struck gold. One of us who now walked with the gods, who was recognised at literary functions, who wiped his backside on quilted tissue and probably changed his pants four times a day, like Prince. *What if...?* we thought to ourselves. *What if...?*

Any similarity between this poem and the everyday reality of being Joe Dunthorne is purely coincidental. He is a lovely man and a fine writer. Probably.

tartlets and raspberry leaf tea – no, that's what managers are for.

You? You'd just *have* one. A delicatessen. *Your* delicatessen. Think about it.

Free cheese for life.

No more own-brand cheddar; no Friday night fight for Philadelphia in the reduced – not for you, matey. Yours is now the world of sunblushed red peppers in chilli-steeped olive oil. Rye bread. Capers. All on tap.

Things'd be different, wouldn't they?
A poet with a delicatessen.

You'd do a gig. They don't like your stuff? You wouldn't be bothered; you'd just smile and take your time, soothed by the warmth of your secret. You might even blurt it out, your words soaring like exotic birds above their bored philistine heads: *I'VE GOT A DELICATESSEN.*

And what a delicatessen! You'd do Poetry Crisps in flavours like *Country Churchyard* and *Sadness of Midnight Trains.* Your mackerel would be smoked in Golden Virginia exhaled through the ruby lips of a waitress who dreams of a career in physical theatre.

On quiet days, you'd burst into your delicatessen.

You'd burst in just to go and look at your staff. *YOUR STAFF*. Imagine you being able to say those words! You who spent your life scribbling in the sad, cold night. You who drank warm Vimto and rolled dog-end fags; who braved the rejection slip and the open mic. *Your staff*. You'd walk amongst them. You'd stroke their beards, touch their printed calico aprons. You'd say, *Don't worry, you beautiful people. As long as I am alive, you will all have well-paid, fulfilling employment.* You'd pay well above minimum wage. You'd maybe even set some of them free, for you are a poet and you like to think you understand the importance of dreams.

And some days you'd just slip into your delicatessen; slip in unnoticed, in amongst the punters in their Superdry gilets, their off-road pushchairs. And you'd take a jar of olives off the straw-dusted, recycled-wine-crate shelves and you'd walk to the middle of the room. And you'd lift the jar above your head; you'd lift it and you'd drop it and it would smash and the world would stand still. And the water and the olives would flood like blood across the reclaimed oak flooring and all eyes would follow the lid as it rolled and flopped and shivered to silence like a hubcap in a movie car-crash.

And the staff would say nothing, because it's you.

And the punters would all look scared and awkward because a madman is obviously loose in the refined environment of an artisanal delicatessen, yet the staff are saying and doing nothing.

And you would walk to the door with slow deliberate footsteps that echoed like gunshots and at the doorway you'd stop. And you'd turn. *You*. The *poet*. The also-ran. The lame duck on showbiz's golden pond. You'd stop and you'd turn and they'd all be looking at you, apprehensive and expectant. And you'd shrug and you'd smile; maybe you'd laugh like Christopher Lee in *The Wicker Man*, a wild-haired god surveying the world you've created.

Just because you could.

Because it's *your* fucking delicatessen.

SAD CASE

I'm on the number 38 to Clapton Pond,
and we're just turning off the Balls Pond Road
when Mick Jagger comes bounding up the stairs,
slumps down in the seat next to me,
an Iceland carrier bag clutched to his lap,
the revealing lingerie of thin polythene
barely concealing the plump oven chips within.[13]

The baseball cap pulled low over his eyes
was pointless. I mean, who thinks *eyes*
when they think Mick?
The *lips* were there for all to see.
Lips that slopped around Mick Jagger's face
like two fat sausages slapped on a grainy bun
by a cocksure teenager.[14]

Those lips. *That* pout. *That* poise. *Those* legs.

---

13   It's all about sex with Mick. Even the frozen goods.

14   Precision in language is everything in poetry. Hard to believe,
     but in the first draft of this poem, I was foolish enough to
     write 'petulant teenager' instead of 'cocksure teenager'. I
     didn't sleep for three nights.

There's only one Mick Jagger
and the top deck were on to him like wolves.

Hey. It's Mick.
Hey Mick, go on, say It's only rock 'n' roll but I like it.
Hey Mick. 'Street Fighting Man'?
That could be about me, Mick.
Hey Mick. Me and my Dolly first had it off
to 'Brown Sugar'.
Hey Mick. Go on, tell us about Keef
and the shepherd's pie. Does he lose it if you break
the crust, Mick? Does he lose it?
Hey Mick, sign my tits with this biro.
Go on, Mick. Go on, Mick.
Mick. Mick. Mick.

Two youths in Chelsea shirts
start up a beery *Sat-is-fac-shun*

And when the conductor comes round,
asking for tickets and passes
he waves away Mick's Oyster card,
just struts off down the aisle,
hands on hips
and Mick grabs hold of my hand,
like a frightened child
grabbing hold of his mother.

And when I say, *I'm sorry, mate. I'm sorry.*

I can't help you. I wake up each morning
meaning nothing to no one,
he just looks at me.

And a single hot tear
falls from Michael Philip Jagger's
unremarkable eyes
and melts a tiny, pure river
through the frost
on his oven chips.[15]

---

15 You see them all from the top of this bus; all the sad cases,
    desperate to undo the Faustian deal. Longing for normality.
    Aching for the thrill of a tube delay, the buzz of knowing
    the price of milk in a range of retail outlets. McCartney in
    the launderette; Rod in the Mare Street Kebab & Grill; Sting
    fondling spuds in Dalston Market. Attempting to be mundane,
    their faces masks of misery as the flashbulbs pop around them.

IN THE BOGS AT THE POWERHAUS

I look up
and I'm surprised to find
I'm urinating next to John O'Neill,
the guitarist from the Undertones.

Life's strange magic has drawn us together
here, in this dim dungeon

and I can't help but stare at him,
but he stares straight ahead
at the chipped black wall,
covered in torn stickers
from eighties indie bands.

I know it's too much to hope
that he will stare back at me,
or thank me if I tell him
how much he means to me,
how *precious* our seconds together are,
and he won't welcome me turning round
and shaking his hand, because his hand
is holding his penis.

So we just stand there,
micturating in the stiff silence
of social convention

and it's left to our urine,
merging uninhibited

in the trough below,
to celebrate this
serendipity –

the piss of a nobody
and the piss that wrote
Teenage Kicks –

swirling joyously together,
shouldering a sodden fag end
and dancing off down the porcelain,
into the strange sunset
of the Islington drains.

IAIN DUNCAN SMITH

The day Iain Duncan Smith
comes waltzing into Connie's Caff
and gets himself a tea, it would have to be
my table he decides to sit at.

No sooner has he parked his arse than he's off.
Being Iain Duncan Smith.
Fixing me with those dead eyes
and reaching right across the table
to snatch the salt.

Mine, he says.

Then he grabs the brown sauce, the ketchup,
the vinegar, the pepper and the mayonnaise, too –
encircles the whole fleet of condiments
with his besuited arms and hauls the lot
across the table and off into his lap.

All mine.

I don't breakfast with MPs. Is this the deal?

IDS slurps from his tea. *Tosser*, he says.

I smile awkwardly.
I'm not a confrontational man.
I'm the one who'd get the post-it notes
stuck on his blazer back:
Kick Me. And everyone did.

It seems the world is out to take advantage,
but I try to *understand* people.
So I try to understand him.
I try to understand Iain Duncan Smith.

Maybe he had that weird baldy
receding hair thing as a kid, too?
They'd have given him hell.
Slaphead, Glans, Bellend:
relentless.
Perhaps that all got too much
Perhaps he grew to hate his imperfections.
Perhaps he grew to hate all imperfection.
Perhaps he grew to hate us: the imperfect.
The unbeautiful. The poor. The unfortunate.

I try my best understanding face.

But IDS just shoots out a hand,
grabs a fistful of my chips
and crams them into his mouth
like a toddler, bits of squashed chip
oozing between his fingers.

This is how I roll, he says
through a mouth full of stolen potato.
This is just how I roll.

Then he slaps me smartly on both cheeks
and tells me to mind his tea;
he's going for a piss.

And he's off.

And, like I say, I'm not a confrontational man
and sometimes it seems the world
is out to take advantage
and sometimes people just don't make sense
and sometimes it seems people
don't want to be understood
and this makes me feel hopeless and sad

and so it is with an infinite sadness
coursing through me like a slow, cold river
that I turn my back to the counter,
unzip my fly and dunk my cock
in Iain Duncan Smith's teacup.

Because sometimes you've got to do *something,*
haven't you?

The discreet bogey in the classmate's dinner.
The landlady's toothbrush up your arse.
Stirring Iain Duncan Smith's tea with your penis.

It feels good.[16]

---

16 The act, not the hot tea.

NIHILIST

Keen to put sparkle back into our relationship, I became a nihilist. I bought a leather armchair and took to sitting in a cloud of tobacco smoke, hawking grolleys into the fireplace and ridiculing Alice's every pronouncement in a thick French accent. *I care nothing for this shit,* I would say when she informed me Mother had called, or asked what I fancied for supper, or hinted she was thinking about lilac for the bathroom.

It worked a treat. My new air of unpredictability lent us a fresh urgency between the sheets, and Alice revealed a touching vulnerability, asking if I still loved her as I lit up a Gauloise and began my post-coital muttering. *Love is nothing but lust and insecurity,* I'd reply. Sometimes I'd get carried away, denouncing the whole bourgeois dead-end of monogamy and suggesting we instead become libertines.

After a month, I came home to find her in bed with Alan and Hester from next door. *Oh, hello,* she said, propping herself up on a perfect elbow. *You were right about the monogamy stuff. I can't believe we bothered for so long.*

I was horrified. *But... but I love you,* I wailed, and began to cry. They all pulled faces and started giggling. *Booorr-ring!* said Alice, rolling her eyes. Hester made the 'Loser' sign, and Alan yawned and wiped my girlfriend's lipstick from his thigh with the sleeve of my dressing gown.

HOMEMADE

In a homemade shed
shaped like a human heart
I drink homemade wine
and write homemade poetry,
tinkering these little worlds into being.

The shelves are old wood out of skips
and on them are stacked a thousand
dead tobacco tins, stuffed
with bits that want to find a use –
hinges, pins, nails, screws,
assorted bits of wire.

Poetry has its own stack of tins –
one marked *MELANCHOLY* is full of station clocks
beneath which no lovers have ever met.
There's a tin of *KISSES THAT FEEL LIKE ENDINGS*,
one for *RIVERS THAT ARE REALLY SYMBOLS*
and lots of birds: *RAVENS, CROWS,*
but they get used up quick,
like *FOXES, WOLVES, CATS, LIONS* –
no sooner in than out with those.

Digging around the back,
I find one tin, forgotten,
rusted shut.

GIRAFFES.

When did you last see a giraffe in a poem?
I prise off the lid. There is just one giraffe.
A bit moth-eaten. Neglected.
I dust him off. Look, *giraffe*.

Run free in *this* poem.

He looks happy.

The power of the poet –
to liberate the oppressed

A minute later, I find something
jammed in a crack of the shelving.

Look. It's Hitler.

I don't want *him* hanging about in the shed.
He can go in this poem, too.

He looks furious.
Not so much the Big Man now, eh?
Not exactly Nuremburg, is it?
Winding up in a poem like this.

No *context*. No *meaning*.

The power of the poet –
to liberate the oppressed and
to bring down the tyrant,
to condemn a dictator
to the prison of a poem.

Immortality with just a giraffe for company.

They look at each other across
the emptiness of the page.

The Führer furiously staring out a happy giraffe.

A fucking giraffe.

Awkward. Clumsy. Odd.
An insult to the Master Race!
Almost like somewhere, somewhen,
some homemade god
just found a neck
left over in a tin
and used it up.

SUBURB

I am to do a performance to a group of retired people in a day centre in a quiet suburb near Coventry. Arriving early, I park in front of the butcher's shop in a small 1960s shopping arcade. The shop has *REAL MEAT* written in uneven capital letters on the window. I can see the butcher sharpening knives and eyeing me suspiciously, as do a row of elderly ladies seated beneath those big helmet hair dryer things in the salon next door.

An aged couple slowly emerge from the door of Kay's Ladies' Fashions. The husband is bent beneath the weight of a bulging Kay's Ladies' Fashions bag; his wife totters beside him, empty handed. Is this the helpfulness of a doting husband – a sharing of life's burdens, as I hope perhaps these two have shared life's joys? Or is it simply that the purchases are his?

The butcher continues to sharpen knives. The old dears beneath the dryers continue to stare.

I take out my notebook and make a rough list of subjects on which I have poems, assessing suitability for this occasion. The list reads:

Revolution – NO
Masturbation – NO
Death – YES
Boredom – YES
Transvestism – POSSIBLY

RELIGION.

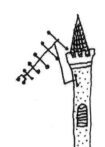

I'LL FUCKING DO THE LOT OF YOU, said God, slamming his pint on the bar and whirling to face the sniggerer. No fucker laughed at the cut of *his* robe. The table of queens went quiet. Someone said *Get her!* under their breath.

I SWEAR IT, I'LL FUCKING DO YOU! ALL OF YOU!

Easy, mate – this was the Devil – *leave it, or you'll end up where I am.*

He put a hand around God's shoulders and tried to steer him towards the door. God shook him off. *FUCK OFF.* He'd just spent six fucking long days creating the world, and now he was resting. He was resting large. A woman at the next table – a hen party – stood up.

Why don't you just LEAVE THEM ALONE, you prick?

The women cheered and sniggered and wiggled their little fingers at God. God wheeled round.

I'LL FUCKING DO THE LOT OF YOU AS WELL, YOU SLAGS.

Come on, mate, said the Devil, grabbing God as he lunged toward the ladies. *Come on. Time to go.*

And he pulled God out the door, God still pointing and snarling, damning all the women and the gays.

MEETING GOD

The Day I Met God it was a Wednesday, after school; War Day at Nigel's. War would happen upstairs in Nigel's bedroom as Nigel's mother – vicar's wife, plump and shy, brown frock and brow-beaten, air of threadbare Nerys Hughes – made tea for us downstairs. *Sossies, chips and beans,* she'd say, *sure and certain as the Saviour's love.*

Nigel would take down the squadron of plastic planes that hung from his ceiling and I would take from my bag my solitary Airfix Spitfire with one wheel missing, and the rituals of Wednesday War would commence. No even-handed battle, this; Nigel had God on his side. God and Messerschmitt; God and Lancaster, Halifax, Lightning Mk V and Vulcan bomber. I just had my Spitfire. Even distribution of aircraft was out. *My planes,* Nigel pointed out. *My planes. My rules.*

Combat was thus brief and inglorious; dogfighting round the bedroom before, inevitably, I'd succumb to Nigel's superior arsenal and nose-dive to the floor in a hail of machine-guns and phlegm.

But this Wednesday, this one Wednesday, I didn't. Perhaps I'd simply had enough; perhaps it was something else, but, as we swooped and whirled through our time-worn steps, this time the Spitfire with the missing wheel refused to be beaten. Nigel's planes swooped from all sides; rat-a-tats, whooshes and kabooms spat ferocious from his mouth, but my little plane weaved unscathed through the impossible wall of flak.

Why don't you fucking die? You've got to die. I've hit you a million times.

But these things happen, Nigel! These things happen! Maybe it's a fucking miracle!

And suddenly, astoundingly, the Merlin engine in that little plastic Spitfire roared into life. That tiny aeroplane just *came alive*; the acceleration jerked me off my feet and up I went. Up and up, trailing behind my outstretched arm like a Kandinsky dreamer as the ceiling split apart and blazing white light flooded the room. Nigel howled below.

This is faith, Nigel! I laughed. *You should understand, mate! This is fucking FAITH!*

I soared up, advancing into the impossible brightness of the light. Out of the house. Above the village. Up and up, until at last, out of that brightness, fellow aircraft appeared. Ramshackle biplanes; patchworked crates, scarred and ragged but still somehow flying. An escort of angels. A squadron of the meek. The pilots all bearing bruises; the bruises of bullied children and broken wives, of battered workers, exhausted and downtrodden; all with heartbreak etched in their tired eyes. And they came toward *me*, welcomed *me* amongst them, and at their helm was Ian Beale in a little red Tiger Moth. He saluted, and together we all banked round in that exhilarating whiteness.

And that's when we saw him. There. HIM. God. A huge, great bearded immensity, lounging in a tracksuit on a giant purple sofa and swearing at David Attenborough on a flatscreen TV of impossible dimensions.

We began our approach to a runway laid out amid the telly remotes and torn Rizla packets on his almighty coffee table. The meek, come to claim our corner of paradise. God glanced up and saw us, and a flash of irritation lit his cold, hard eyes. He pointed straight at me, shaking his head. *Not you,* he shouted. *Not you. Your name's not on the list. No name on the list, no fucking entry,* and, grabbing a remote, he aimed it at me and jabbed with his thumb.

And then there I was. Back on earth. Back in Kingshill. Back sprawled on Nigel's carpet, clutching a broken plastic Spitfire with one missing wheel. And Nigel stood over me, shaking his head, panting, a bomber clenched in the fist of each outstretched arm. I could taste blood in my mouth.

And Nigel's mother called up that tea was ready. Sossies, chips and beans. Sure and certain as the Saviour's love.

GRID REF. S.U. 877 979.

EXCERPTS FROM AN IMAGINARY
RE-IMAGINING OF THE ARSE END
OF NOWHERE (LT. KINGSHILL, BUCKS.)

INTRODUCTION

I was a born *flâneur* and a natural psychogeographer from an early age. Unconsciously at first, of course – merely responding to an inner compulsion to walk, to observe, to immerse myself in the lie of the local land; in its flora and fauna, its history, its development. To try to find some sense of belonging, sort of oneness with what was – as my memorable felt-tipped contribution to the Where We Live wall display in Mrs Perrett's class put it – a *dull and shopless outer-suburban Metroland shithole.*

Only after discovering a copy of Guy Debord's legendary Marxist-Situationist art-as-revolutionary-theory bible *The Society of the Spectacle* tucked between the Enid Blyton and *Gumdrop Rides Again* in Missenden village library did I begin to formalise my approach. I smuggled this slim volume in through our House Checkpoint concealed within my Panini *Football '78* sticker album and, as Father cast protective spells over his defensive worldview by reciting Baden-Powell's speeches backwards over *These You Have Loved*, I surreptitiously devoured it on the sofa.

I was instantly hooked. Like Debord in post-war Paris, I too longed to redefine and reimagine my stultifying environment: this hell of pleasant lanes and half-arsed topiary, of Scout huts and old ladies selling reasonably-priced eggs from cottage doors. The next day, as Mrs Pegley the librarian slipped the orange ticket back into the book and gave me my smiley sticker for being a Good Returner, I demanded everything the little library had to offer in the way of Situationist and proto-psychogeographic texts. For the next three weeks I buried myself in the word and lore of esoteric topography, and I still clearly remember the moment – *Roobarb* on the telly; Mother cutting up my fish fingers – when I resolved to do for Little Kingshill what Walter Benjamin had tried to do for the arcades of nineteenth-century Paris.

From that point on, my German shepherd dog, Tulyar, and I would never again concern ourselves with the banality of 'walkies'. Instead, we set out daily on *derives*: unplanned 'drifts' through the village and its environs, opening ourselves to the whims and pulls of the subconscious; to the subtle authoritarian manipulations of parish council neighbourhood improvements. I found myself drawn to narrow paths and neglected corners, to overgrown farm machinery and to 'power spots' – the concrete pad on which the vicar fixed his Land Rover; the knoll from which Old Mrs Heather threw stones at children. Tulyar was drawn to dog piss and bins.

I found I wasn't alone. I soon crossed paths with other junior psychogeographers. Wary, but cordial, we'd often meet on local benches, carving *I LOVE LIMINAL SPACE* into the faded wood and sharing custard creams, French fags and strategies for subjective intimacy with

Place. Just occasionally would things turn nasty – a squabble over who invented Will Self; a punch-up for psychic dominion over the energy node of Thames Water's Deep Mill Pumping Station – and we would part company, reminded of the essentially solitary travails of The Walker.

Thus bit by bit, walk by walk, I pursued My Project: the creation of an exhaustive three-dimensional mind-map of my locale from a logged and catalogued grid of Emotional Node points. From the trauma zone of the school gate to the rite-of-passage spot in the hedge by the common where we found a dead rabbit, to the T-junction where I'd once fired a pea-shooter at the local mod. I came to dream of the village, to be assailed by its collective memory, to be woken screaming by nameless horrors lost deep in its history. Bit by bit, walk by walk, I flowed through Little Kingshill, and Little Kingshill began to flow through me.

1. LITTLE KINGSHILL

i.

Ride the long purple arm of the Metropolitan
right out to the empty fist of Amersham,

then fifteen flint-filled fields where pylons limp
like refugees across the Chiltern scarp
toward the bleak exile of the Oxford plain
and you're there.

ii.

You'll note retriever dogs squat on gravel drives
smug as Hitler's tanks on the conquered streets of
Warsaw: idiot sphinxes guarding mausoleums of
    the living,
the cherry orchards now but logs and memories.

You'll see the ghost of Betjeman,
astride his golden bicycle
like a triumphant field-marshal,
coasting down neat lanes lined
with mock-Tudor newbuilds knocked up
for the overspill of the post-war boomtime dream.

Listen. Hear the warm wind waft the muffled-whump
drumbeat of slammed chest-freezers, the porcelain
laughter of moneyed twats playing tennis.

26. VEGICIDE

Watch Dad rock up in his Hillman Avenger
tooled up for Saturday's war.
These gardens are little Vietnams.

Now watch the bastard *go*.

Watch him crawl on hands and knees,
flushing out weeds like cornered partisans.

See how he lives the dream!

The Homebase Rambo;
no guns and no grenades,
just a cold, clear iron will,
a mud-smeared screwdriver
and a tub of Fisons' Lawn Doctor.

39. YOUTH CLUB

Was a bone-cold Baptist church hall, sixties brick and stark fluorescents.

Was plastic bucket chairs lined up like Light Ent celebs to cup the soft buttocks of Kingshill's crop of under-twelves.

Was Authority. Was Mr Price: lay preacher; lanky Führer; coal-black, cold, black[17] Come-to-Jesus eyes strobing out through bottle-end glasses.

Was God's disgust with the tightness of Joel Bailey's Sta-Prest trousers.

Was *KerPlunk* and *Connect 4* on Formica tables scrawled with spurting cocks by God-baiting virgins from cul-de-sacs.

Was breath steaming on chill air; was a tinny record player and a Woolworths-stickered stack of seven-inch singles.

Was Authority's disapproval of Adam Ant and eyelinered men in general.

---

17   These four words in this order are shamelessly stolen from Under Milk Wood, and are included purely to set off the irritating alarm sound on Ira Lightman's laptop.

Was tuck shop and the hedonism of retail. Was fingering Black Jacks and fondling foam bananas; was eyeing soft, pink candy shrimps that sang of fecund oceans far removed from landlocked little lives.

Youth Club was all these things; was cold air and God's wrath; was board games and records and cheap confectionery.

But mostly Youth Club was Alison Giles.

Alison Giles! Your plump and creamy bramble-scratched Girl Guide thighs shrinkwrapped in a tease of torn denim... Alison! Tomboy-charmed and urchin-haired, swimming badges stitched to green trackie top... Alison! It wasn't lust. We knew nothing of lust. We were too young and it wasn't that kind of village. Alison! It was more than that your father worked for the railway... I felt things, *indefinable* things... Alison! That time after tuck shop you gifted me a fistful of those candy shrimps, hot and sweaty from your palm and I sat in my chair, my eyes tracing the contours of your full calves, the open pores boreholes down which I longed to dive, hungry to understand the mechanisms, the tectonics of woman beneath your scabbed and chalky skin...

Youth Club was Alison Giles,
was my hand alive to the firm, warm,

damp pinkness of her gifted sweets,
was feeling things I couldn't understand,
was Authority's searchlight eyes
boring through my soul,
was condensing breath
clouding above my head
like sin.

57. SEX

We discovered sex beneath an elder tree on the edge of the common. It was a mucky magazine. Trevor took it home and, after prolonged study, claimed to have learned its secrets. He told us appalling things. Waterlogged and mildewed, faded and torn, the magazine was indecipherable to me. My impression of sex was shaved wrestlers struggling in mist; the aroma of leaves and piss.

It remained that way for years.

66. SCHOOL: HOW THE NAZIS HAPPENED

I shat my pants in primary school.[18]
I locked myself in a toilet cubicle,
discharged my foul cargo and missed the pan.
It flopped like a corpse on the cold, pink tiled floor.

The crime was quickly discovered.

I joined the rubberneckers, jostling
to glimpse the evil glinting in the half-light,
this grotesque queen to a hive of giggles
and whispered theories

I reckon James Morley did it, I said,
knowing I'd be on to a winner.
It was swiftly picked up as a chant:
James Morley! James Morley!

Even the caretaker pitched in, brandishing his
bucket and mop like an am-dram crusader.
James Morley, he nodded, as he bent to his task.
Aye, he does those...

---

18   This illustrates perfectly the importance of correct wording
     in poetry. I shat my pants in primary school: obviously a
     reminiscence. I shat my pants in a primary school: that's
     different. The inclusion of the indefinite article changes it from
     reminiscence to status update.

As I step down into the playground, James Morley,
all carrot hair, snot and awkwardness,
is being dragged from breaktime marbles by
tough blond nine-year-olds from Mrs Perrett's class.

He is crying *I didn't do it! I didn't do it!*
and as Mrs Massey strides up, lips pursed,
looking like she means business, I turn away,

pull my hands from my pockets,
begin counting up the swapsies
from my *Football '78.*[19]

---

19   Even now I can remember them all: Arsenal's Liam Brady
      and Malcolm Macdonald, Terry McDermott of Liverpool,
      Spurs manager Keith Burkinshaw, his grinning Argentinian
      striker Osvaldo Ardiles and three of Mick Mills, the veteran
      Ipswich Town captain. All of their faces in my memory wear
      expressions of undisguised contempt for my cowardice and
      irresponsibility – the Mills triplets especially, unsmiling and
      with coppers' moustaches, look like they want nothing better
      than to kick my spineless little head in, down some Suffolk
      alley.

68. THE PSYCHOGEOGRAPHER RETURNS

I AM LITTLE KINGSHILL,
I announce, stood in the kitchen doorway
and breathing heavily.

Look at my hair, wet with Chiltern rain
and dyed the fire-red of Chiltern beech in autumn.
Look at my tweed, torn on Chiltern hawthorn;
my trousers, stained with Chiltern chalk
and the dog shit of pedigree Labradors.
I have consorted with mosses in Haleacre Wood
in thrall to the mushroom god;
I have slept afternoons beneath the hedge
by the fizzing omphalos of the electricity transformer.
My shoulders stoop
from years as your own paper boy,
bent beneath my glossy orange bag
and the weight of lifestyle supplements
and right-wing opinion.

I AM LITTLE KINGSHILL.
I am the fucking spirit of this place.
I am a son of this place.
I am one with this place.

My mother looks at me uncertainly.

My father asks if I have found a job yet.

74. HOME

Interned behind locked double-glazing,
that's me: slumped at the kitchen table
gazing at the back of the Weetabix pack
where the gang of cartoon skinheads
shout of a world of camaraderie and casual
    violence;
of opportunity and fun as distant as
the Heathrow jets that rumble ceaselessly overhead.

Are cartoon skinheads a good way
to advertise Weetabix?
Do cartoon skinheads imply
that Weetabix is no-nonsense?
Do cartoon skinheads imply
that Weetabix is aggressively proletarian
and that this is an attractive quality?
Or are cartoon skinheads simply
a coded admission that Weetabix
is offensive to the majority of the population?

I have no answers to these questions,
or to a million others.
For I am not yet a man of the world;

just a child of the A413 corridor.[20]
Slumped at the kitchen table
in a house in Little Kingshill,
in the parish of Little Missenden.
Two pubs, one school, no shop.
Known to estate agents as *desirable*
and to us as home.

---

20 This line is a tribute to the ex-*Take a Break* sub-editor and
    greatest comedian-that-never-was, Duncan Bolt, who said
    something similar in a workshop I was helping run before
    he turned his back on the world of comedy and returned to
    ambling around North London in a duffel coat. I couldn't bear
    to see the line die, unloved and unheard. But it might only work
    in his voice.

BOOKS & RECORDS

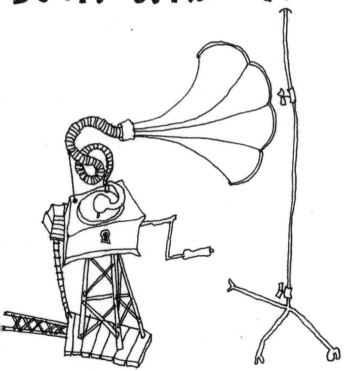

POEM FOR JEFF THE HIGH WYCOMBE SHAMAN

THey say that music is magic.
A band CAN change your life;
that much I know.

But someone has to show the path, Jeff;
someone has to take your hand. Someone
opens the door. And each time ~~XXXXXXX~~
~~XXXXXXXXXXXXXXXXXXXXXXXXXXXXXXX~~ I found
myself walking up the A404 with rain
pissing down my neck, a bagful of records
and no bus fare, it was you.

It was you, Jeff.
You were like my anti-matter dad,
doling out nuggets of second-hand wisdom
all carefully-graded and
competitively-priced.

It was you. The DJ at the funeral of
all my mother's hope; you'd wrap my
downfall in a bag and as I sloped off
you'd recommend the latest seven-inch
from some no-hope mohawked vegans
from Leeds, and how could I say no, Jeff?
You had such strong, strong juju.

And I? I was just a chalked-stained
Chiltern lad when I first pushed past your
poster-plastered portal, first caught that
fag-and-incense smell; my pockets burning
with the earnings from saturdays-from-hell
in the garden centre of a moon-faced racist.
Raised on You And Yours and Marmite,
I was running and I fell into your arms.
Your arms, and your record shop, Jeff.

SCORPION RECORDS

Scorpion was my temple. It was my church.
And you, Jeff- ensconced in your pulpit
beneath a votive tableau of a thousand
sun-bleached button badges- you were
the priest.You omphalos of hipster otherness.
You jazz druid. You released in the boil
of my hormonal fluids an unshakeable power.

Perhaps it's better to say
you gave me a gift: one of
the greatest gifts a man can give.
The gift of Musical Reference Points.

You gave me guiding lights, Jeff
to burn brightly in the agonies of night.
You gave anchors to calm my ship in a storm.
You planted unshakeable rocks,
sacred stones scattered like bones
about the bleak terrain of my inner landscape.
You gave me power places. Safe spots,
and lots of them.

Look- there's Steve Ignorant from Crass,
stoking the bonfires of my anger.

There's Captain Beefheart, for when
I wish to appear difficult.

And up on that unstable promontory,
there's Morrissey, waving his daffodils
and spouting brittle poetry.

These and so many others,
they are an army I carry within me.

So women, come and do your worst:
Jeff's voodoo cocoons me like a shield.

And yea, though I walk through
the valley of middle age
I will fear no evil: for as Paul Simon
had his books and his poetry to protect him,
so I have my books and my poetry
AND my extensive record collection.
And so I fear nothing.

NOTHING.

Not women.

Not life.

Not even Paul Simon.

BOOKS AND RECORDS

It was Johnny Thunders who said
You can't put your arms around a memory.
He was right.

And you can't put your heart
around a download

and you can't fall in love
with a digital information package.

But books and records, that's different.

I love books and I love records. *Paper* books. *Vinyl*
records. I love them, hold them and feel them.

Books and records are more than just *stuff.*

Hoovers and kettles and bathmats and gloves are stuff.

Books and records are more than that.

Books and records sit on their shelves above my desk.
My walls are propped up by an extra wall;
a wall of books and records.

Eight hundred multi-coloured bricks of knowledge and
wisdom and feeling. Eight hundred imaginations. Eight
hundred lives that stand between me and the woman
next door who shouts at the hissing eye of her television.

I collect books and records.
And books and records collect me.
They are living things.

The books are me.
They age and fade and come apart
and slowly stain and scar
just as I stain and scar and fade and come apart.

The records are me.
Played and dropped and scuffed and scratched;
lives lived round and round
in ever-decreasing predetermined circles
until one day they warp and die
and there is some small sadness
in a tiny corner of the world
and life moves on.

I cannot put my record player on shuffle.
Every listen is a deliberate act,
a conscious interaction.

A memory stick
can hold more words than the largest book
but you try resting your paper on a memory stick
to write a love letter.

Every book and every record has made its mark on me,
even if that mark is the mark of complete indifference.
I cannot imagine what such a mark looks like, but it is
there. Every book and every record has made its mark

and I have made my mark on it; it has offered up its magic and that magic lives on somewhere deep inside of me.

Books and records.

I collect them and they collect me. They are sucking up my life.

The books are all scrapbooks of my moments.
The books have our times together
mapped out in fingerprints
and the kiss of breath trapped in the papery fibres.

Knut Hamsun wears turmeric stains from an awkward samosa.
Dostoyevsky sports crusted kisses from the lips of bedtime yoghurts.
Richard Brautigan is flecked with spots of morning coffee from a summertime in Brighton; gifts dripped from one moustache to another.

The toast crumbs, with and without Marmite. The distant perfume of the girlfriend whose stockinged foot dislodged my bedtime bookmark. The midnight tears and all the Vimto spilled in anger. The aroma from long weeks lost beneath the pants of the broken-hearted.

I push on through the darkness, guided by the light of books, and my love scars them with a thousand dog-eared corners and a hundred broken spines.

I push on through the darkness, buoyed by the music of
records, and the crude magic of a diamond stylus scuffs
a patina of surface noise; layer upon layer of clicks and
pops that gradually ghost my presence in these records'
lives.

Party times, drunk in charge of the record deck.
The night jumping round the flat with Molly
to *My Favourite Dress* that wound up
jumping the needle forever.

That week after Sophie left,
when *Whole Wide World* took a battering,
play after play after play and sadness
gouged its rough moan deep into the plastic.

Books and records.
Every day they take more souvenirs;
a disorganised diary of undated damage
every time I have turned to a book
or reached for a record.
The happy times.
The sad times.
The times when it was raining outside
and it felt like I had nothing better to do.

The Richard Scarry books
I loved to pieces when I was four.

Novelty singles from childhood and the seven-inch of
Space Oddity donated by the uncle who worked in the

record business that exploded in our suburban bubble like a declaration of war from another universe. And every one of the thousands since.

Books and records:
we have marked each other indelibly. They are cursed to bear my molecules forever just as I cannot unhear shit music or unread shit prose. Each scuff, each stain, each crackle and buzz is the co-ordinates of a moment marked on the evolving map of my existence.

When I die, if you joined up all these plotted points, perhaps they would make great leylines across the emptiness where I used to be. Perhaps they would spell out the word *LIFE* in giant letters beyond the constraints of time and space. Or perhaps they would just make a giant indecipherable scribble, senseless and subtly upsetting.

Perhaps that is the same thing.

If I die before my books and records, let them hold an exhibition. My body will be laid out, bloated with spent life. My books will spread themselves open, inviting children to lick the pages and learn the sad secrets of the grown-ups. The worn vinyl will blast out my life in a symphony of white noise; a strange Morse code through which, if you listen closely, you will just make out a half-familiar tune.

No- Fi Stand-up Spoken Word Theatre

MAN UP, JONNY FLUFFYPUNK

ONE MAN'S STRUGGLE WITH LATE-ONSET RESPONSIBILITY

STAGE YOUR OWN PERFORMANCE
Full instructions included

FULL 1 HR. SHOW

EVERYTHING INCLUDED!

MAN UP, JONNY FLUFFYPUNK[21]

A cheap workbench[22] is on stage. Not a deluxe Black & Decker adjustable height model. Oh, no. More the £16.99 Homebase own-brand version. A small, vintage cardboard suitcase is on top, with a miniature clip-on desk lamp attached, and beside that, front stage right corner of the workbench, are some pots of poster paint, a brush and a small modelling vice. Attached to the wall behind, at head height, is a washing line, with clothes pegs/bulldog clips. Jonny ENTERS picking out a sparse, bleak, repetitive motif on a banjolele. He is a fraction under six foot, which rankles him deeper than it should. He is slim, but we're talking awkward and

---

21   I was originally going to call this show *Jonny Fluffypunk Searches for the Hero Inside Himself... Then Goes to Bed Disappointed*. But what is that save taking the flag of failure and running it straight to the top of the mast, where it hangs limp in the wind of public indifference? And this is not about failure.

22   Not, alas, the solid wooden magnificence your granddad had in his shed, which is what *everyone* understands by 'workbench'. We're talking about the flimsy folding metal thing with the winding handles that was invented and popularised by Black & Decker in the seventies. But they've trademarked the name. So I'm not allowed to write 'Workmate' here when referring to the cheapo copies you get in Homebase. So I have to say 'workbench'. Luckily, however, Black & Decker rarely turn up to see what I do at gigs.

unsavoury rather than elegant; more old man Steptoe than early Bowie. He is wearing off-white gentleman's combinations (which he is already regretting, given the heat of theatre lights), heavily darned and stained officer's breeches, full-calf woollen puttees and World War I ammunition boots. A rolled-up oatmeal balaclava is on his head. He has an Edwardian moustache and, more by accident than design, is probably unshaven. He gazes at the audience in wonder.

Ah... people![23] Good evening. I am Jonny Fluffypunk, stand-up poet and sustainable nihilist.

Welcome to my shed *(Jonny indicates the symbolic, MANLY workbench)* and this show, *Man Up, Jonny Fluffypunk... One Man's Struggle with Late-Onset Responsibility...* we start with an opening contextualising piece...

Jonny pulls a toy accordion from the suitcase and launches into the following story, punctuated at irregular intervals with a recurring accordion riff. Performance veers from understated to desperate and impassioned, and act as a primer for the audience as

---

23 This opening two-word salvo is delivered with what reviewers naïvely assume to be feigned surprise. It is, however, a crucially important moment in establishing a low-status relationship with the audience, usually enhanced by their meagre numbers.

to what to expect from the unprepossessing figure stood
before them, in whom they have invested the price of a
couple of pints and an hour of their time.

Mum wore the trousers in our house. And what
trousers! Vast, buff, land-girl corduroys against which
her buttocks strained with playful mystery, like a
giftwrapped moon.

Father had to assert his displaced maleness
elsewhere. So, at the top of the loft ladder, in the
cobwebbed recesses of the attic, he built himself an
empire. A kingdom of papier-mâché hills and fusewire
trees, of resin lakes and cardboard villages through
which 00 scale trains rattled his tiny dreams to termini
of the imagination. It was a peaceful and law-abiding
kingdom, and Father held dominion from his control
panel at the centre, a Brylcreemed Führer in station
master's hat and Paris-cut combinations, running his
fingers over the point switches and control knobs,
feeling at their tips the electric hum of power.
But one day something happened. Exactly what, we never
knew. A Friday night kick-off in one of the cardboard
pubs? An indecency behind the clip-together Hornby
engine shed? Whatever; the law-abiding tranquility had
been shattered by an act of social deviance and Father's
response was swift and remorseless.

My brothers and I were summoned from
downstairs to bear witness and, in Father's words, learn
something, and we stood, shoulder to shoulder, playing
with ourselves and each other through our pyjama

pockets for comfort as Father raged at his fallen Eden. With a swagger stick whittled from the thigh-bone of a conscientious objector, Father drove the tiny 1/76th-scale plastic villagers from their homes so that they gathered, huddled in terrified knots, in gardens, village squares and fields as above them their god unleashed his fury, a Benzedrine Gulliver at war with a Lilliput that had betrayed him.

'You ungrateful bastards!'

Father's sausage fingers swooped down like sweaty zeppelins and scooped at random men, women and children, those whom he would make a bloody example of. And they were marched, heads bowed, up the steep slopes of the biggest papier-mâché hill and there, at the top, without ceremony, trial or mercy, Father strung them up from fishwire nooses hung from the fusewire trees. Then he struck a match from a box of Swans kept beneath his hat and held it beneath the crotch of one of his tiny, twitching victims. With an evil hiss, a wreath of foul black smoke twisted tortuously upward against the endless, pitiless sunset of the forty-watt attic bulb.

A terrible silence fell. We turned, prisoners of our thoughts, and shuffled away; the remaining little villagers back to their sad homes, my brothers and I back downstairs. And in the womb of my bedroom my heart broke for those miniature plastic victims, and for victims of savage authority everywhere, and I wept. I wept and I wept and something died in me that evening; an innocence was lost. At last I turned to my bedside

shrine, removed the effigy of Valerie Singleton –
moulded from wax and hair and real human teeth – and
with hot, angry hands remoulded it into one of Mick
Jones from the Clash.

And then I slept. And I awoke an anarchist...[24]

Right, so that opening contextualising piece is there
to establish broad themes of father/son relationships,
radical politics and the fallout from dysfunctional
families.[25] So, yes, welcome to the show; actually, I'm
visualising it more as an *expedition* than a show[26] – an
expedition to find the source of self-worth for a man
lost at the beginning of a new and bewildering digital
age. And not just a man, but a father. Which, experience
reveals, means *'man on almost continuous trial'*. Now
this show isn't exclusively about fathers, or for fathers,
but fathers *are* awarded an elevated status... and as we
are going on an expedition together, I need to know the

---

24   This piece first appeared in my last book. Don't feel cheated;
       see it more as collecting all the formats. This is the album
       version. It sounds different to the version in the other book.

25   Themes which, it has been pointed out by at least one critic,
       I 'hammer into the audience subconscious like nails of
       unresolved trauma hammered into a bewildered but ever-
       trusting puppy'.

26   At this point I indicate my stage apparel, thereby revealing
       to the audience that the breeches, puttees and trench-boot
       ensemble is not just a sex thing.

strengths of my team. That's you. *My team*. So, do we have any fathers here?[27]

Jonny pulls from his pocket a handful of military-style MEDALS (FIG. 1). It is immediately obvious that they are made with cardboard, coloured paper, felt tips and safety pins. He hands out the 'Dad' medals to whatever fathers in the audience have put their hands up, while speaking the following line.

FIG. 1: DAD MEDAL

safety pin's gotta taped to reverse

DAD ★

A small cardboard medal.
A Dad medal. Small recompense for the years cleaning sick out of car seatbelts; for all the money stolen from your wallets.

Jonny indicates fathers in the audience with a heroic sweep of the hand, and becomes loud and impassioned. Desperate, even. With hints of bitterness, regret and faded dreams. A snapshot of the real man behind the

---

27   There will usually be at least one father in the audience, though often they are reluctant to admit to it. Remember that they may only be in your audience to get a bit of peace; a few fragile moments to themselves. In these cases, your precious spoken word theatre show is simply a semi-cultured alternative to locking oneself in the khazi with the paper. Also, the more harassed, broken and unenthusiastic the fathers, the better. For our purposes, if not for their children.

charismatic legend we know and love. This is backstory conveyed in a cracked vowel; in a pause that lingers a second too long. This is show, don't tell. This is fucking ART.

Look at them, people... men you want to trust. MEN YOU WANT TO BELIEVE IN.

Jonny activates the foot switch for the tape recorder, which plays the same simple banjolele riff that was played 'live' as the performer entered. If Jonny happened to know more than four chords, this might all be improved upon.

Retreating behind his workbench, he dons two sock puppets. Jonny gives the impression that he is unsure about what is going to happen and is mustering his meagre resources to take the plunge; few acting skills are required here. One puppet has a moustache and a beret. The other has a tie, a pair of glasses and receding hair à la Mr Burns from the Simpsons, conveying an air

of retirement.[28] The bereted puppet is chirpy and eager; an innocent. He is obviously intended to be Jonny. We'll

---

28   The moustached sock puppet is a homunculus of Jonny Fluffypunk (and should be adjusted to suit the peculiarities of the performer). The other puppet is meant to be my father, though I have gone for more of a 'generic' old person look as my own father is nondescript.

call the puppet JFP. The one with the glasses is airily disdainful. The Father. Jonny (the performer) comes back out to centre stage, the puppets working the room – the JFP puppet perkily, the Father puppet surveying room, stage set and audience with contempt. The foot switch is stamped on in a confrontational manner – the performer is on the defensive again. He's at the mercy of these fucking puppets. The music stops. Pause.

Father: What is all this, son?

JFP: It's a show, Dad... a show about me. *Man Up, Jonny Fluffypunk.*

Father: *(quietly mocking)* Fluffypunk... what kind of a bloody name is that?[29]

JFP: *(ploughing on regardless)* It's about me, about being a man. It's about inadequacy. 'Will I make it?' Father: *(contemptuous)* You? *'Make it'?*

JFP: Will I make it as a dad? That's the jeopardy. The *tension.* Qualified, yes, to argue gender politics over a pint in the snug bar of the Parasite's Arms *(Father puppet nods, sadly),* but *qualified to shape a young life?*

---

29   The father puppet also has a northern accent. My real father is not northern, but I've found it's the easiest way to 'do' disparaging.

Both socks look at each other, then slowly, doubtfully, back at the audience.

JFP: I'm a dad now, Dad. I'm on a pedestal. I'm a... a *role model.*

Father: *(slowly looks from audience to the JFP puppet, then to the human performer, then slowly back to the audience)* Jesus Christ.

There is a long, static pause. Then Jonny – crestfallen – slowly removes puppets and returns them to the suitcase. He looks winded, and lost, as if he has forgotten he is in the middle of a theatrical presentation. At last he snaps from this reverie, and, as if trying to re-establish himself, becomes suddenly and briefly loud and hammy.

SO... this is an expedition conducted entirely via the medium of lo-fi spoken word theatre! Now, every expedition needs a vessel, transport for the journey, so throughout the show I thought I would build us A SHIP! (Jonny takes the small, crudely-whittled wooden hull of a ship from the suitcase and clamps it into the vice whilst speaking) A little ship, for the epic voyage of manhood![30]

Then Jonny seizes the paints and brush from the workbench, brandishing them with the air of a Picasso.

So, what colour are we going to paint it? Come on, this is a group decision...

Once a colour suggestion is extracted from the wary audience, Jonny roughly slaps paint on wooden boat whilst continuing to talk.

It's important YOU made that decision. It's symbolic;

---

30   The sniggers that inevitably greet the revealing of the little wooden boat are there to be played with to the performer's advantage. The audience – typically, pseudo-cultural hipster barflies with no concept of the intimate relationship between craftsman and material – think they're *better* than this performer and his hamfisted creativity. They do not understand that I am deliberately provoking their mockery; that I am simply obtaining free fuel for the throbbing engine of defensiveness which propels the show. And which later will backfire in their uncomprehending faces.

symbolic of the fact that we're in this together. This is not a *spectacle*; this is not a performer performing AT an audience. This is performer and audience in fragile symbiosis. This is an expedition. I'm the captain. You're the crew. We're like Jason and the Argonauts, but instead of the technicolour Aegean, we're in *(Jonny here inserts a derogatory description of the venue).*

So... *an expedition* by spoken word theatre. People ask me, what is this new genre, this 'spoken word' we keep hearing about? Well, in this case spoken word is a fusion of poetry without any discernible rhyme or rhythm and stand-up comedy without any discernible jokes. But they're flinging money at it. The *Arts People*. Flinging money at spoken word. Spoken word on Broadway. Spoken word selling out the Old Vic[31]. People keep telling me *I* should go for it. Go big. After all, it's a big theme, isn't it? 'Being a Man'. 'What's *THAT*?' they say. *(Jonny indicates the boat in a derisive manner)* 'What's *THAT*? If you were doing *proper* spoken word, if you were doing it *properly*, you'd be collaborating with a cutting-edge hip-hop dance troupe. *They'd* build a giant, impressive *proper* ship across the back of the stage, whilst rocking improvised moves involving power tools and sundry discount DIY products.'

---

31 It's not often I find myself thus – astride the cultural zeitgeist; a bargain-bin fairy atop the Christmas tree of opportunity and hard cash.

Jonny stares challengingly at the audience in defensive posture; there is an element of shame, but also of fierce pride – fuck generic cliché and fuck hip-hop; I MADE THIS BOAT! Jonny draws the awkward silence out as long as possible.[32]

OK, so I've *provided* you with a vessel *(points at embryonic wooden boat)*. Now, we'll also need a map. Here it is, our map *(pulls out MAP (FIG. 2))*. A map of the next fifty minutes, complete with waymarked points, colour-coded. Bits marked with blue 'X's indicate poems – scripted, well-tested material. They work. We're *safe* there. These areas in red *(indicates vast majority of the MAP)*... they're the danger areas. The Uncharted Territory of the Now; the show as it unfolds with you, this audience, tonight. We're in the realm of the unknown. How well it goes depends on how well we work together. It could be joyous. Like a cruise on sultry summer seas. Or it could feel like we're trapped in a living hell, drinking our own urine and praying for the blessed release of death. Depends on how well we gel as a team. It's up to you. So... *(indicates points on MAP)* we've done 'Opening Contextualising Device'... we've done 'Connect with Dads' and 'Sock Puppets #1'. Now we're on 'This Map Bit'. This bit coming

---

32   This is easy for me. I love awkward silences, just as I love
       kneejerk defensiveness. They remind me of home. And family.
       If you're a fan of awkward silences, then stick with this show –
       you're in for a treat.

up is 'Delegate Task to the Crew'. That involves *you*. And on it goes, towards one of two possible endings. Either we end together, on the beach at sunset (*Jonny indicates one end point*). Or I drown alone all at sea (*Jonny indicates the other end point, then hangs MAP on washing line*). If anyone feels lost at any point in the show, feel free to come up to the front and consult this...

FIG 2: MAP

Of course, this map only represents the *physical journey*. It is of course also an *emotional journey*. So here's an Appropriate Emotional Responses diagram.

Jonny reveals amusing EMOTIONAL RESPONSES DIAGRAM (FIG. 3) – a cardboard-and-felt-tip graph featuring an unsteady line with a marked peak at beginning and end and a marked trough in the middle.

FIG 3:
EMOTIONAL RESPONSES DIAGRAM

The x-axis represents the ongoing progression of the show. The y-axis represents your enjoyment of the show based on known limits of human tolerance. As you can see, there's an initial early rush of excitement, reaching a crescendo *here*... that's where I first opened my mouth... then it's very up and down. Now this *here (indicates the marked trough)*... all art is subjective. Each of you will find your own personal hell. You may find that this one is not to scale. It's quite short... Then there's this final upswing *here* where you know you'll now be able to go to the toilet, to breathe fresh air, to live again.[33]

Jonny hangs up EMOTIONAL RESPONSES DIAGRAM on washing line.

So, we are equipped.

Our expedition starts, of course, in childhood, for if fatherhood is about setting an example, then childhood is where one *learns* the example, as I did from my father. My father, who would retire of an evening to his Empire Room – his cubby hole beyond the fridge-freezer and the washing machine – where he would recline on the chaise longue beneath the world wall-

---

33   Although it appears to be little more than a digression, a comic setpiece, the inclusion of the emotional responses diagram shrewdly places on the stage an emergency recovery device for the performer and indeed the show. To extend the journey-by-ship metaphor of the show, this is one of those red lifesaver rings beside a dangerous weir. Should things go tits-up later – typically during the Nestor Makhno/anarcho-communism routine, when the audience frequently becomes visibly bored and resentful – then suddenly picking up the diagram and pointing to the 'low point' instantly results in tension-releasing laughter: a necessary acknowledgement that both performer and audience are sharing the pain.

map still coloured two-thirds empire red, beneath his watercoloured etchings of natives subdued at the butt-end of a Lee-Enfield rifle, and read to us from his leather-bound library of 'Top Hole' stories and 'Deeds That Thrilled'; read to us of Grand Gestures and Great Men.

Men like Captain Matthew Webb, first man to swim the Channel *(Jonny reveals CAPTAIN WEBB PICTURE* (FIG. 4))*. Thirty-nine miles in twenty-two hours. It's only twenty-one miles to France. *That's* not good enough. So he zig-zagged, pausing every two hours for a half of ale and a sausage. A hitherto

FIG 4: CAPTAIN WEBB

impossible physical feat, accomplished whilst drinking six pints and eating eleven takeaways. Captain Webb, *a British hero.*

Jonny hangs CAPTAIN WEBB PICTURE on washing line.

Men like Ernest Shackleton's 1914 *Endurance* expedition to the South Pole *(Jonny reveals PICTURE of SHACKLETON's team, lantern-jawed and rugged in chunky knits and balaclavas* (FIG. 5))*. Ship sunk, crushed by polar ice, but to a man they survived, crossing the world's most treacherous ocean – navigating only by the stars – in an improvised rowing boat hewn in sub-zero conditions by the ship's carpenter, who put aside his grudge against Shackleton for shooting his pet cat, Mrs Chippy.

FIG 5: SHACKLETON'S TEAM

Jonny hangs SHACKLETON PICTURE on washing line.

This was the world my father surrounded himself with; a world o tough men. A world of empire and certainty; *his shield against a changing world he couldn't hope to understand.*[34] A changing world of Boy George and Channel 4, of lesbians on Greenham Common and soap operas on the BBC.

And now it's my turn. Now *I'm* the father. Two little boys: Ianto aged seven, Percy aged two... This is a poem about the birth of my first son. 'My Son Is Born'.

---

34 This line needs to be emphasised. It's an important callback, imparting (by the end) a sense of a circle completed; a resolution of sorts.

Jonny picks up banjolele, then interrupts himself, suddenly in bitterly defensive mode again – achieved by visualising himself standing atop a colourful mountain of Arts Funding leaflets, all bearing the tagline 'Are YOU aged 16-25?'

Of course if I was doing spoken word *properly* I wouldn't have this *(Jonny indicates banjolele)*, would I? I'd have a group of beatboxers... what is the collective noun for beatboxers? *(pause for response)* I'd have a *(inserts elicited collective noun)* of beatboxers, not this banjolele, and the beatboxers I'd have symbolically dressed as members of Shackleton's team, trying to make hi-hat and snare noises through thick woollen polar mufflers, symbolising Man pitting himself against seemingly insurmountable obstacles...

Jonny once more 'rides' the silence, wringing a thin milk of pity from the withered udder of the audience, then recovers a vestige of assertiveness and resumes banjolele picking.

My Son Is Born[35]

Born in the middle of a wet Welsh May night,
dark and unappetising as burnt barabrith,

---

35   This particular poem was written during a difficult phase, when I became possessed by the spirit of Dylan Thomas.

as drizzle drummed on hard slate roofs,
drizzle chattered wetly in the gutters and gullies,
drizzle that babbled and burbled the news –
in an old slate-miner's cottage, my son is born.
My son is born...
My son is...

There is a long, awkward pause.

Yes, well, that one needs finishing. That's the problem with having children. You *start* a project and...

FIG 6: TWO SONS: PHOTO

When I told my children I was doing this show, I asked my eldest son if he could do me a portrait of himself and his brother, so I could contextualise them for the audience. He said, 'Yes, Dad. I'll do you a portrait.' Here's the portrait he did.

Jonny reveals PORTRAIT OF TWO BOYS (FIG. 6). *The PORTRAIT is obviously a computer-enhanced digital photograph.*

As you can see, the chosen medium for the portrait is SLR digital photography with Photoshop image manipulation. This took him fifteen seconds. *Fifteen seconds!* And you know how? Because he's a digital native. That's what they call them now, the children. *Digital natives.*

Jonny pegs PORTRAIT to washing line.

I'm not a digital native. I've done my own portrait of them, using a more traditionalist approach.

Jonny reveals his PORTRAIT 2 (FIG. 7) *of the two children, amusingly rendered in the spidery, primitivist, felt-tip style associated with four-year-olds.*

FIG 7 : TWO SONS: TRAD. DRAWING

I know what you're thinking...
He's just homaging Dubuffet.[36]
But this didn't take fifteen seconds.
This took *FIFTEEN YEARS*
(becomes aggressive). Fifteen years mastering the entire Western artistic canon before I was qualified to cast it all aside and paint with the untutored simplicity of a child. *FIFTEEN YEARS.* Fifteen years in which *I GREW AS A MAN.* You don't get *that* with Photoshop.

Jonny hangs up PORTRAIT 2 on washing line. He considers it, then turns to audience.

Two children who look to their father as I looked to

---

36   The audience always seems to laugh at this line. I find this
      reassuring – that a spoken word audience seems familiar with
      the work of French 'outsider art' guru Jean Dubuffet. Possibly
      they're confused and think they've heard him freestyle with
      Raekwon and Method Man.

my father, as he looked to his father... as children have looked to their fathers throughout time. AS A GOD. As an unquestioned *god*.

Jonny waits for someone in the audience to laugh, so they can be rounded on. Frequently nobody laughs. In which case he can round on the whole audience.[37]

Not how *you* look at me... THEY LOOK ON ME AS A GOD.

But my son came up to me with his iPod – his grandmother, his *mamgu*[38], she gave him an iPod... ten minutes to master it; half an hour to break it. And he said, 'Daddy, fix it! Fix it, Dad. Fixer Man! GOD!'

For this last exhortation, Jonny breaks out of the little scene he is enacting and addresses the word with a mixture of triumph, venom and despair at someone in the audience who had laughed at the initial 'God' claim. Then there follows an extended mime of a helpless, clueless man faced with an impenetrable, sealed plastic box and a child radiating complete faith.

---

37   Standing, chest thrust forward, in front of a sparse Fringe theatre audience dressed like a fool whilst trying to convince myself that my children look upon me as a god is basically my life in a nutshell. Authenticity is all. Happily for the show, however, it also continues to reinforce the idea of a desperate and deluded man.

38   My eldest son is half Welsh. The half I don't understand.

'Son, I can't... I can't fix it... it's not even got screw holes... it's... it's... it's DEAD PLASTIC.' *(Jonny suddenly rounds on the audience)* Look how disempowered Daddy is! *(The next lines are delivered almost as a babble, such is the despair)* You've got this little organism that looks at you with complete and utter belief, with trust and love, selflessly giving the gift of their faith, and in exchange for this precious gift, what do these two get? They get a poet for a dad. Whoopie doo. *A poet*; a feckless artiste. *They* give me the unconditional gift of faith; *I give them a Petrarchan sonnet workshop.*

This is the recurring nightmare. At home, at night, in my poet's garret, pulling my sparse, thin poet's 3.5-tog duvet tight around my sparse, thin poet's body, I toss and turn on the bare wooden boards[39] and night after night I'm in the grip of it. In my mind's eye their little faces are like little upturned bowls, crying out for a dad – a *proper* dad. A dad like in the Heinz adverts when I was a kid, in front of a crackling fire, a cardiganed icon of reassurance – to ladle in the thick, nourishing soup for the soul: the potatoes of wisdom, the carrots of knowledge, the peas of... whatever.

But instead he gets me, the *poet* dad, up in his ivory tower, leaning from the window and dribbling the lukewarm broth of disappointment.

---

39   Yes, the poet sleeps on bare floorboards. Mattresses are the
      vain affectation of novelists.

But I won't be a disappointment. Not to *them* as well...

As he concludes this soliloquy with a flourish of bravado, Jonny stamps on his foot switch and the familiar banjolele riff cranks out. Jonny walks behind the workbench and once again pulls on his sock puppets, this time with a demonstrable mixture of reluctance, trepidation and resignation to the requirements of the show he has regrettably embarked upon. After a lengthy pause, he visibly steels himself and returns to centre stage, warily eyeing the Father puppet as if it has both a life of its own and – like the real thing – a propensity to piss on artistic endeavour from a great height. Jonny stamps the foot switch and there is silence. And a pause.

Father: Oh, you have it *hard*, son.

JFP: Well, try being a bit bloody supportive.[40]

Father: Oh, that's right, you stick the boot into your old dad.

JFP: I'm not sticking the boot into you!

Father: Well... why are we here, then, son?

JFP: I just explained all that.

Father: No, why are *we* here? Us? S*ock puppets*?

JFP: *(looking sheepish)* Well...

Father: Son, I get the feeling I'm being used as a Brechtian device.

---

40   These sections of the show are both comedy as art and Gestalt therapy as a spectator sport.

JFP slowly hangs his head.

Father: I'm being employed as a non-naturalistic theatrical conceit[41] symbolising an overbearing authority figure conveniently responsible for a lifetime of crushing under-achievement.

JFP: *Well... (a bit affronted, but basically caught out)*

Father: Seamus Heaney, son... Seamus Heaney put *his* dad in *his* poems. *Seamus'* dad gets to symbolise the continuity of tradition, the importance of family. *(Shouting now)* SEAMUS HEANEY'S DAD NOBLY DIGS POTATOES.

JFP hangs his head in shame.

Father: Oh, don't worry, son. You haven't disappointed me.

JFP puppet looks hopeful.

Father: I had no bloody faith in the first place.

At this point, Jonny the performer takes on the hurt and affront of the JFP puppet, as the boundary between show and reality starts to blur even more than it already has. The performer drops his JFP puppet hand,

---

41   See – there are jobs.

but continues staring at the Father puppet, with an inscrutable expression that hints at the deep complexities of approval and betrayal that underpin the father/son relationship. It is a sad and poignant moment, and it is shamelessly milked. Jonny suddenly snaps out of it, and angrily flings the puppets into the suitcase, before remembering where he is and attempting a painfully obvious 'on with the show' attitude.

So, yes – our boat! Er, so now we add the mast, symbolising thrusting... on...

So, what *is* a man? A few things I did take from my dad: a love of steam trains. An appreciation of George Formby. A replica pith helmet. The acute financial acumen? I gave that one a miss.

FIG 8: TYNDALE-BISCOE OF KASHMIR

And I took this book: the autobiography of this man, Canon Tyndale-Biscoe of Kashmir (*Jonny reveals PICTURE of TYNDALE-BISCOE (FIG. 8), which he attaches to the washing line as he continues talking*), celebrated Victorian educationalist and celebrated MAKER OF MEN.

Jonny then removes BOOK – the autobiography TYNDALE-BISCOE OF KASHMIR – from the suitcase and holds it aloft as he continues.

My father raised us from this book, quoting aloud as

my brothers and I covertly held erection competitions in our pyjamas for the coveted prize of pressing cold spoons onto the back of Mother's calves to ease the throb of her varicose veins.

And this was the chapter he quoted from. Not this one, 'Fuzzy-Wuzzy', not 'A Gross Case of Cruelty', not 'Profiteering and Child Murder', but this one, 'Character-Building'[42]. For Tyndale-Biscoe believed men were *made*, not born. That by following a few simple instructions, and with rigorous discipline, then – from the most unprepossessing of raw materials – one could fashion A MAN. So my father would photocopy out these charts – Tyndale Biscoe's Boy's Character Sheets *(Jonny slings BOOK to floor and reveals photocopied and enlarged character-building CHART (FIG. 9))*[43] – attach them to the fridge with his novelty Ted Heath nudie fridge magnet, and award my brothers and me points for such things as 'ABSENCE OF DIRTY TRICKS', 'COLOUR OF HEART', and 'PLUCK, UNSELFISHNESS AND GOOD TEMPER'.

Jonny attaches CHART to washing line.

---

42 These are genuine chapter titles. The book also features interesting photographs, such as the one of non-swimming youths being flung from third-storey windows into Dal Lake in Srinagar, the theory being that they then had better bloody well learn to swim. And quick.

43 Again, these are genuine charts from the book.

FIG 9: CHARACTER BUILDING CHART

Boy's Character Form Sheet

Each boy has a page in the register to himself, and three times in the year his character is overhauled and written down thus:

Name _____ Son of _____ Entered Central School _____ Class _____ 194 . Entered _____ 194 . Branch School

Roll No. _____ Ocçn. of { Guardian / Father _____ " _____ Class _____ Left _____ 194 . Left _____ 194 .

Date of Birth _____ Date of Marriage _____ Father's Salary

Date	Class	Item		Full marks		
		Age				
		Average Age of Class				
		Position in Class				
		Ears and Throat				
		Eyesight				
		Teeth				
		Height				
		Weight				
		Chest Measurement				
		General Health				
		Tutor				
		MIND — English		150		
		Urdu or Hindi		150		
		Persian or Sanskrit		150		
		Science and Drawing		300		
		Mathematics		150		
		History		150		
		Geography } or Physiology / Hygiene		150		
		Calligraphy		100		
		General Knowledge		300		
		Total		1,600		
		BODY — Gymnastics		400		
		Boxing		200		
		Swimming		200		
		Headers		100		
		Games : cricket, football, etc.		200		
		Manual Labour		100		
		Total		1,200		
		SOUL — Scripture		200		
		CONDUCT TOWARDS Masters — Obedience, Respect-fulness, Truthfulness and Honesty		400		
		Boys — Pluck, Unselfishness and Good Temper		300		
		Esprit de Corps — School		300		
		Duty to Neighbours — City		300		
		Colour of Heart*				
		Total		1,500		
		MANNERS — Deportment		200		
		Absence of Dirty Tricks		100		
		Self-control		100		
		Total		400		
		DISCIPLINE — Cleanliness { Body / Clothes and Tidiness		200		
		Attendance		100		
		Punctuality		100		
		Total		400		
		Grand Total		5,100		
		Signature of Principal				
		Remarks				

* We have eighteen shades between white and black. More Boys, thank God! become lighter in colour each year, if not each term.

* The result to the true boy is a recommendation, to the other condemnation. When a boy considers that he has not been treated fairly I never put down my signature until the boy assents to the truth of the marking. I have met one or two boys who have considered themselves too highly marked. by his teachers, the whole class is asked to decide the question.

And through such means my father sought to make us into men. Now, what Tyndale-Biscoe believed made a man could be boiled down to three basic precepts: Leadership and Strength of Character; Physical Prowess; Honesty and Commitment to Truth.

Jonny indicates PLACARD (FIG. 10) *in front of the workbench, emblazoned with these noble principles.*

So, Leadership and Strength of Character... well, I'm *leading* you, aren't I? This is an expedition; I'm the captain, you're the crew. I'm handing out medals, willy-nilly... that's a *leadership* thing, isn't it? And I'll tell you what else is leadership... delegation! I can delegate... remember, on our map? 'Delegate Task to the Crew'?

So, there's this saying... this African saying... this traditional African saying... this ancient, traditional, African saying that says... 'It takes a village to raise a child'. Sadly it turned out under close investigation

that this ancient, traditional African saying was made up by Hillary Clinton to help sell a self-help manual *but*, real or not, I really like that cynically-invented ancient, traditional, African saying, because it embodies important principles of mutual aid and cooperation, of collective effort. Principles I hold dear. It is a good *example* – and being a good leader, a good *father*, is about setting a good *example*. Now, I don't have a village, but I do have this small, self-selecting cabaret audience. This is *community*, and you will play an instrumental role in the raising of my children. I am *delegating*. Like a *real leader...* so, I want simple words of wisdom. *Your* wisdom. On this paper *(Jonny pulls out CLIPBOARD and PEN from suitcase)* it's got written *DON'T FEAR THE WORLD, JUST REMEMBER...* over and over again, with gaps. The gaps are for you to write your wisdom.[44] So, I want you to circulate this. Fathers in the audience, I'm expecting you to keep an eye on things.

So, Leadership... my father gave me examples to live by.

Jonny indicates Captain WEBB and Ernest SHACKLETON PICTURES on the washing line.

---

44   Time and again I would have to supply a new pen, because audience members would steal them. Eventually, I tied the pen to the clipboard with string. And when that wasn't enough, I glued the pen to the string with a glue gun. It's a sad indictment when a culturally-aware, theatregoing audience sees fit to steal a felt tip forty minutes into a show by, and about, a desperate, self-deluding man at the mercy of his own inadequacies and the dictates of society. No wonder George Osborne is running riot.

I want to give *my* sons an example. And who better an example than *this* man?

FIG 11: COMRADE NESTOR MAKHNO

Jonny reveals MAKHNO PICTURE (FIG. 11), then takes the picture and strides assertively into the audience. This is his pet subject.

Does anyone know who this man is?[45] *(pause)* This is Comrade Nestor Makhno, Ukrainian peasant revolutionary of the early twentieth century.

Russian revolution, 1917... picture the dreary, oppressive landscape cowed under the thick black cloud of Tsarist rule... picture the thunder of Bolshevik revolution;

---

45   No one ever does. Except a Polish woman in Southampton, who berated me afterwards for hero-worshipping the man she claims liquidated her family in 1921.

more black clouds but with a sort of reddish tinge... but in southern Ukraine, Comrade Nestor Makhno breaks through all these clouds like an impudent golden sun; a sun that warms the spirit of the people and raises a peasant army that establishes in southern Ukraine for several years an autonomous anarchist republic...

Jonny returns to stage and hangs MAKHNO PICTURE on washing line.

Nestor Makhno... what a leader. What charisma... I teach my sons about him. I teach them via the medium of a fun family bedtime game, where we all huddle together beneath woefully inadequate bedding and enjoy a lucky dip of pertinent historical facts about Comrade Nestor Makhno, all culled from Comrade Arshinov's definitive *History of the Makhnovist Movement 1918–1921.*

I thought we might re-create the fun here in this improvised theatre environment.

Jonny fetches a pack of playing cards from the suitcase. The conceit is that the playing cards all have a pertinent historical fact attached to them, though for the purposes of the show there only need to be three fact-attached cards. (The audience doesn't need to know that, though Jonny's clumsy hunting for the requisite card for the purposes of the show normally gives the game away. In which case, Jonny cleverly passes this off as a 'knowing' meta-theatre deconstruction.) Jonny approaches the audience, brandishing his cards.

OK... pick a number... any number between one and fifty-two...

Whatever number is shouted out is irrelevant; Jonny reads from labelled card #1. This is repeated twice more, using the random selection of three FACTS (FIG. 12). For standard comedic purposes, it helps if fact #1 and fact #3 are in some way funny, and fact #2 is dry and tedious. If feeling perverse, this can be jumbled up, creating a genuine awkwardness and sense that things have gone badly adrift. To be fair, even if following the 'standard comedic' fact pattern, there's still usually a sense that something has gone badly adrift. There seems to be a universal lack of interest in the minutiae of pre-Soviet populist insurrection and applied anarcho-communism. You fools.

Anyway, this particular section of the show should gradually grind to a halt. The wheels have come off, and we're up to the axles in the mud of awkward tension.

To be honest, the family is usually asleep by now... I don't really know... ummm. We've kind of gone up a blind creek, expedition-wise...

Jonny is suddenly seized by inspiration and pulls a small cardboard rudder from the suitcase, which he proceeds to fit to the boat.

A rudder, symbolising my unerring sense of direction...

FACTS (FIG. 12).

1. Comrade Makhno earned the nickname Batko, or 'Little Father', amongst the troops after a fighting retreat in September 1918, in which Makhno and thirty partisans, cornered in a forest and considering individual escape beneath their revolutionary dignity, fought their way past a full regiment of the Tsar's army, who – despite overwhelming odds in their favour – fled in a panic to the Volchya river, where enthusiastic peasants drowned them.

2. At the beginning of 1919 the Makhnovist insurgents, having thrown back Denikin's troops toward the Sea of Azov after a hard fight, captured a hundred carloads of wheat from them. The first thought of Makhno and the staff of the insurgent army was to send this booty to the starving workers of Moscow and Petrograd. This idea was enthusiastically accepted by the mass of insurgents. The hundred carloads of wheat were delivered to Petrograd and Moscow, accompanied by a Makhnovist delegation which was very warmly received by the Moscow Soviet.

3. Whilst entrenched outside the town of Gulyai-Polye, Comrade Makhno and Comrade Schus disguised themselves as Ukrainian peasant girls, the better to infiltrate behind the enemy position. Although concentrating on counting out rounds of ammunition, Makhno couldn't help but notice how pleasant the soft linen of the undergarments felt against his battle-hardened soldier's skin, and – not for the first time – it crossed his mind how lovely it would be to be a woman. Turning on his newly-commandeered heels, Comrade Makhno tottered up and down the ranks of his ragbag army, gazing into the eyes of the men, making sure no one had a fucking problem with this. The men had to try hard not to laugh, for Makhno had spilled a little of his lunchtime Borscht ration (a Ukrainian beetroot soup) down his chin; attempts to wipe it away had resulted in smearing which, combined with his feminine attire, made him look like a cheap Kiev prostitute.

He intones the chant:

The wind whistled, the wind blew, the foam flecked and the foam flew and the captain and his ragbag crew sail on, on, on, over the seas of... man.

Jonny indicates the 'Noble Principles' PLACARD.

So... Physical Prowess... OK... *(looks as unprepossessing as possible)* this one I'll admit I'm having difficulty with. How to prove my physical prowess within the confines of an improvised theatre space... it did occur to me that perhaps the best thing to do at this point would be to offer to fight someone in the audience... anyone? *(pause)* I toyed briefly with the idea of a rug, so we could wrestle like Oliver Reed in that film. A wrestle on a ragged rug... a ragged-rug wrestle with a poet... of course, if I were doing *proper* spoken word... if I was doing it *properly*, then at this point the cutting-edge urban hip-hop dance troupe could wheel on an inflatable boxing ring and they'd all be wearing silver silk shorts emblazoned with a printed motif of Poet Laureate Carol Ann Duffy's snarling face.[46]

---

46 The use of Duffy's face on the shorts is deliberately populist. Early versions of the show had me dress my hypothetical hip-hop dancers in 'hi-cut briefs embossed with the frowning visage of Cambridge avant-gardist JH Prynne', but this image, although provoking laughter from the cognoscenti, was met mainly with uncomprehending looks. Thus leaving my dancers, conceptually speaking, standing awkward and embarrassed,

Any takers? *(pause)* Perhaps someone a bit inadequate, perhaps someone out with a lady...[47] perhaps they think they'd like to impress their partner and friends by beating up a poet... SPOILS THE SHOW for everyone else, doesn't it? BUT WHAT DOES THAT MATTER, EH?

Jonny suddenly softens and perhaps even smiles warmly at any audience member he has been briefly bullying.

And then it was pointed out to me that I don't *actually* have to fight *anyone*. And you know why? Because I'm a poet. And I have nothing to prove. For a poet is inherently dangerous.

I AM DANGEROUS.

And yes, I can see you all looking at me... thinking *he's not dangerous*... thinking *that could be me if I lost a few*

---

clad in the unfashionable pants of academic irrelevance.

47 Obviously, if there is someone in the audience who looks inadequate, or is sitting with someone else in a manner reminiscent of an awkward first date (where going to some sort of theatrical presentation seemed like a good idea as you could get to savour and enjoy the smell of a potential new partner without the social minefield of having to talk to them), then they can be homed in on, to their discomfort and the audience's amusement. Though generally I disapprove of that sort of thing.

key social skills, if I forgot how to dress appropriately... but you'd be wrong. I AM DANGEROUS. I am a poet, and it was ever thus. *Mad, bad and dangerous to know,* as Lady Caroline Lamb described Lord George Gordon Byron, and it is still true. I go into schools. I do workshops, putting shapes and colours into the minds of the young, and before they let me through the door, I have to show them a certificate proving that I've got ten million pounds' worth of public liability insurance. *Ten million pounds... TEN... MILLION... POUNDS.* What damage could I do to a child that's worth *ten million pounds?* With *poetry?*

I used to be a carpenter. When I was a carpenter I had to have five million pounds of public liability insurance. That means that somewhere out there, someone thinks I can do TWICE AS MUCH DAMAGE TO YOU WITH A POEM AS I CAN WITH A CIRCULAR SAW.

Jonny stands proud, full of threat and bravado.

Makes you think twice about heckling, eh?[48]

Jonny punches the air, for once full of himself rather

than defensive and cowed. Still punching the air, he walks – nay, he strides – he strides behind the

---

48   You should, of course, never heckle a poet. Each time you
      heckle a poet, somewhere out there Morrissey tries to rap.

workbench and for the third time dons his sock puppets. This time, though, he's the fucking boss. He's yanking them on, smirking triumphantly as he does so. He has nothing to fear from these wool-based bastards. Not this time. He comes out from behind the workbench, the JFP puppet now punching the air. The Father puppet hand is still, however, in its usual position, unmoved by all this bluster and fuss.

Jonny strides up and down the stage with his puppets, working the room. Only gradually does the JFP puppet start to notice that the Father puppet is not joining in with all the strutting and glory. Never mind; in a moment he will! But he doesn't. And the JFP puppet starts to deflate slightly. And then deflates more. For once again it would seem that his father is pissing in Jonny's pint pot. Stamping on the fragile gossamer of embryonic self-esteem.

The JFP puppet is now thoroughly deflated. We're back at square one, as if the whole 'Physical Prowess' routine hadn't happened. We climbed the ladder of unbridled joy only to throw shit dice and slide straight back down the snake, robbed of self-delusion.

Jonny himself is now round-shouldered and broken where moments before he had been cockily erect. There is pain on his face. These puppets are bastards and are back in charge; Jonny is a vessel. Simply a vessel. The JFP puppet suddenly rounds on and snarls at the

Father puppet.

JFP: What is it now, eh? WHAT IS IT NOW?
Father: *(pause)* Is this it?
JFP: What do you mean, *is this it?*
Father: Is this it? Is this 'Being a Man'? Is this what
          it is?

JFP puppet is silent.

Father: Is this *really* it? A man? A man in the twenty-
          first century? Is this it?

*The Father puppet is now warming to his derisive
theme.*

Father: Is this it? P*retending to fight your own
          audience?* That's being a man, is it? *A pretend
          quiz about a dead and forgotten failed
          revolutionary?* That's it, is it? That's *Being a
          Man.* That's *Father Material.* That's...
JFP: *(interrupting)* It's a *show,* Dad. It's a bloody
          show!
Father: Oh... I *see.* A *show.* So... this is the
          entertainer, giving the audience what it
          wants...

The JFP puppet suddenly loses his rag; Father has

mentioned the 'E' word.

JFP: I'm *not* an *entertainer... I'M AN ARTIST!* I'm an artist. I give the audience *what they didn't know they wanted!*

Father: *(distantly)* Oh, is that right... an artist... what have we got next, then?

The Father puppet turns and reads aloud from the 'Noble Principles' PLACARD.

Father: Honesty and Commitment to Truth... *(the Father puppet's tone now turns to one of open derision)* Honesty and Commitment to Truth. HONESTY AND COMMITMENT TO TRUTH... son, you wouldn't know truth if it came up AND BIT YOUR BLOODY BACKSIDE.

Uh-oh. That's done it. The puppets stare at each other. Then slowly, painfully, the whole show falls apart. Jonny's shoulders slump. That puppet has kicked him right in the guts, the machine-knitted little shit. Jonny's puppeting hands fall lifeless, and he swings away, suddenly oblivious to the show, to the audience, to everything. In a sudden movement he wrenches the Father puppet off and flings it to the floor. Then he just keels over, back to the audience. Depending on the venue he might end up in a ball on the floor or leaning against the wall or whatever. The important thing is that his back is to the audience and that he is motionless. He drags this out as long as possible. Certainly far longer than a dramatic pause, or anything that would happen in conventional theatre. The motionlessness is the key – any of that tortured swaying and sighing and it looks like fake shit. Instead this awkwardly starts to look like some sort of genuine mental instability in the performer. Something has gone wrong and we're now off-script. It goes on so long that even the most patient audience starts to whisper and make derisive comments about Jonny's obvious inherent genetic unsuitability as a performing artist and his flawed notions of value-for-money entertainment.

Suddenly Jonny wheels round, puce with rage. Some mechanism has finally snapped. For the next five minutes or so, the audience is on the back foot. Some or all of the lines may be whispered through gritted teeth and directed to the back of the stage; equally, they may be screamed into someone's face from a distance of six inches. Not quite so funny now, eh?

I was gonna to do a *POEM*, right – I was gonna do a simple love poem and then I was going to DECONSTRUCT it; deconstruct it to reveal the truth behind the seemingly innocuous lines. That's what I was going to do... see, it's on the map... but *he's* right *(Jonny wildly indicates the Father puppet, crumpled somewhere on the ground. His voice is wretched in defeat).* HE'S RIGHT. It's not real truth. It's just MORE FUCKING WHIMSY

PRESENTED AS TRUTH.

The following soliloquy, though it may look flat on the page, is delivered with such visceral pain that it comes over like fucking Shakespeare. LOVE ME, it screams; love me and understand me, for I am human, just like you. First, though, there is a long pause. Then Jonny starts quietly, as if exhausted and shellshocked, then increasingly animated. If the truth is going to come out, he thinks, well, you might as well have the WHOLE truth; you despise me anyway.

So... what is truth, then? What is truth? Truth is this, isn't it?

Truth is a forty-six-year-old man struggling to come up with a fitting end to his stupid little show.[49]

Truth is this, isn't it? A forty-six-year-old man who desperately wants to be a Heinz advert dad. An icon of warm reassurance, sat before the crackling fire, ladling nourishing soul-soup: the potatoes of wisdom, the carrots of knowledge, the peas of... whatever...

Truth is this: a forty-six-year-old man, a fo— a MIDDLE-AGED MAN, slumped on the sofa, struggling with similes, wrestling with metaphors as his partner

---

49 Clever, eh? An acknowledgement, right at the key moment of raw honesty and truth, that this might actually be a shrewdly-considered part of a narrative arc. I *told* you being a poet was about danger.

heads off to the night-shift, twelve hours' nursing in A&E, only to return in the morning to find the two boys wailing and begging for breakfast and the middle-aged man still *slumped*, still *struggling*, still *wrestling*, but now beneath the disappointed gaze of his family...

And where's the Heinz dad in *that*, eh? Where's the icon of warm reassurance? Where's *my* soup? Where's *my* potatoes? Where's *my* carrots? My *whatever*? I've not even got a fucking ladle. Just a middle-aged man, slumped on the sofa and clutching a wooden spoon, whilst the brave new world headbutts my front door, its one hand Tweeting a status update, the other... *playing Angry Birds*. And the only crackling fire is the inferno from all the bridges I've burned.

That's *truth*. THAT'S TRUTH.

And I tell you what else; truth is *this*. It's me, Jonny Fluffypunk, naked and alone. Just me. No collaborative hip-hop dance troupe. No posse of beatboxers. No inflatable boxing ring. No PowerPoint projected presentation of forty fun-filled father facts. NOTHING. All that, that's for *other people*. That's for the 16–25 funding bracket.

This is just *me*. Just me and a banjolele, a workbench – not even the expensive Black & Decker multi-level one, just the £16.99 own-brand one... just a suitcase, some wood, felt tips, some cardboard...

Jonny tails off, before delivering the killer line of meta-theatre.

AND AN INCREASINGLY DEFENSIVE STAGE PERSONA... [50]

My shield against a changing world *I* can't hope to understand. [51]

So, not so very different from my father; him cocooned in a world of heroes and empire and certainties, me cocooned with my lo-fi puritanism and my desperate hope for revolution because I've failed to sort a pension scheme. It's come full circle...

The soliloquy is over. There now follows a self-consciously awkward pause. This bit is not scripted. I just need to look lost, adrift and slightly moronic.

---

50   If the audience hasn't been nervously sniggering at the wittily poetic lines scattered throughout the preceding simulated breakdown, then this is the line that finally bursts the tension. That lets them off the hook. Its emphasis and delivery are adjusted according to how hard work/immune to humour the particular audience happens to be.

51   This is that important callback mentioned earlier! It needs a big gap and emphasis. This is the show coming full circle. Suddenly it's NOT just a loosely strung together collection of vaguely funny bits. Suddenly I look clever and like there's a point to it all.

Flapping arms uselessly. Without a script, this is my

default stage presence. When I do at last start talking, it is naturalistic, with as little stagecraft and timing as is possible. Aimlessly wandering the stage is the mode, uttering this sort of thing:

So, it's all gone pear-shaped... tits-up... so, what happens now, then? Where do we... go?

After a bit, Jonny suddenly seizes the banjolele from the floor, as if mustering heroic resolve.

I'll *tell* you what happens now. We CARRY ON. We carry on and we make the fucking best of it. We carry on, because we *have* to carry on. Because I have to carry on. Because I'm DAD, and I can't just go giving up. A dad can't just give up when it goes wrong. *Life* goes wrong, and you just give up. Not when their little soup-bowl faces are gazing expectantly at you from the cold helplessness of the void. I'm Dad and I have to carry on. Because they BELIEVE in me. *Their little faces BELIEVE IN ME!*

Jonny starts picking the banjolele riff we've been hearing all evening, and seamlessly segues from the above ramble into the following poem, which rises in intensity as Jonny talks himself into some sort of ramshackle self-belief.

I am Dad.

I am the surgeon for skinned knees
and the Picasso of Lego.

I am Dad.
I am the genie that rises from the page
and breathes steam into the boiler of Thomas
night after night after night after night after night after
night.

I am Dad
and I am the greatest goalkeeper those boys have ever seen.

I am Dad
and I am the god-bird that circles above
the deep green valleys of childhood;
that cracks open the sky and lets in the light.

I am Dad and I am all these things.
Magic dances from my fingertips
and I talk sense into the universe

I am Dad
and today I am the greasy zookeeper
unlocking the cages of my menagerie –
come on, son, and meet the tools –
the pliers. The wirecutters. The screwdriver.

The adjustable spanner. He eats nuts.

See, son – tickle his tummy, watch
how he opens his jaws.

Because today we are fixing the bicycle –
we are fixing the bicycle that my dad fixed with me
and his dad fixed with him.
And I am taking my son's hand in mine
as my dad took my hand in his
as his dad took his hand; as fathers have taken
their children's hand in theirs, back through time,
a litany of dadnesses: dad after dad after dad
after dad after dad after dad
who took their child's hand in theirs
as I take my son's hand and together
we lift the spanner and tighten the wheel.

Dad! Dad! It's stopped wobbling!

Yes, son. You fixed it.

I fixed it?

You fixed it.

I fixed it... I'm a fixer man. I AM A FIXER MAN?

Yes, son. You are a fixer man.

And he looks down at his hands
and his eyes have that look
that you only see in the eyes
of small children. And astronauts.
As if seeing something for the first time.
As if witnessing a miracle.

And I am Dad
and I am proud to stand by
holding the brushes
and mixing the pigments
as another new artist
paints his world into being...

*Jonny ends and rides the poignant, awkward silence –
often punctuated by sighs and other strangely tender
noises from the audience, because the atmosphere in
the room has collapsed from the affected, manipulative
tension-building and desperation of the first forty
minutes via the raging confessional into something
approaching genuine intimacy.*

So, well... that's my... potato of wisdom... laughing at
my own folly *(Jonny laughs mirthlessly)*... my carrot
of knowledge... basic bicycle maintenance... my peas...
forget the peas... now let's have *your* wisdom. Your
contributions to my children's upbringing... can I have
your participatory sheet back, please...?

Jonny now performs the audience participation sheet

– 'Don't Fear the World, Just Remember...' as a list poem. Typically it is a mixture of heartfelt advice, random oddness and gratuitous sexual content, and appropriate witty asides are made to the audience during the performance. Then Jonny attaches the poem to the boat's mast. Fuck me, it's a sail! At this point the audience usually makes the sort of gentle, affirmative noises you make when absent-mindedly rubbing a cat. If the venue is so equipped, the stage lights now dim to a single spot focussed on the workbench as Jonny lifts the boat off the vice, closes the suitcase lid and places the boat on it, facing into the glow of the desk lamp.

I give these boats to my sons and they love them; a new toy, every night, unique and made by Dad. I put the boats in the bath with them, and they have to learn to fight to save themselves from drowning beneath the accumulation of shoddy tat and well-meaning aphorisms... which is a life lesson, isn't it?

This is my Fathership. Rough and makeshift. Crude and wobbly. A bit crap, really. But always bravely struggling on toward the light, powered by love and poetry. Crewed by you lot, and captained by me, the poet. A man who'll never swim a sea or find a pole or... see a revolution, but who led this small cabaret audience, in a shed, for fifty-five minutes. And no one died. No one walked out. No one even went to the toilet. Not on my watch. A man, not perhaps in Tyndale-Biscoe's mould, but a man nevertheless. Legally speaking, it stands up;

I've looked into it. A man who now stands triumphant, at journey's end, clutching a brace of symbolic root vegetables: the spud of self-deprecation and the carrot of bicycle maintenance, green shoots in the barren allotment of self-worth. *(Jonny bends down and seizes one of the discarded puppets)* And I can look my sons in the eye and say I breathed life into an old sock, and I smote it down. And I can resurrect it... and that, boys, is as close to God as any of us should ever be allowed to get.

And I'd like to leave you with one final example to live by:

Jonny reveals PORTRAIT OF FRANK DAVIES (FIG. 13) and hangs it on washing line.

Private Frank Davies, 2nd Battalion, Monmouthshire Regiment. Killed in action, Western Front, December 1914. Killed in action: shot in the back, by mistake, during the Christmas truce, whilst taking a gift of fags and sponge pudding to the enemy.

Face-down in the dirt and shat on by fate, but still striving to the last moment to commit a little act of beauty in the face of a world gone mad.

Good night.

Jonny bows and exits, if the venue permits it. Or, if

FIG 13: PRIVATE FRANK DAVIES

it doesn't, he just has to stand there. Looking deeply uncomfortable.

THE END

THANKS AND ACKNOWLEDGEMENTS

With special thanks to Clive Birnie, Liv Torc and the Burning Eye crew, Tony Allen, Tony Bennett, Paul and Ros, Dennis Gould, Mr and Mrs Broadbent and their shed, Jo and Neil and all at Stroud Valleys Artspace, and everyone who has put me on, put up with it, come along and just enjoyed any of it. Thank you.